LOST LEAGUE
FOOTBALL GROUNDS

Michael and Drew Heatley

Ian Allan
PUBLISHING

Lost League Football Grounds
Michael & Drew Heatley

First published 2010

ISBN 978 0 7110 3475 3

© Ian Allan Publishing Ltd 2010

Published by Ian Allan Publishing

an imprint of Ian Allan Publishing Ltd, Hersham, Surrey KT12 4RG.
Printed in England by Ian Allan Printing Ltd, Hersham, Surrey KT12 4RG.

Visit the Ian Allan Publishing website at
www.ianallanpublishing.com
Distributed in the United States of America and Canada by BookMasters Distribution Services.

Mixed Sources
Product group from well-managed forests, controlled sources and recycled wood or fibre
www.fsc.org Cert no. SGS-COC-005526
©1996 Forest Stewardship Council
FSC

INTRODUCTION

This book completes a trilogy that started in 1994 with *Football Grounds Then And Now* **(Dial House, out of print) and continued a decade later with** *Football Grounds Fact Book* **(Ian Allan). As its title suggests, this volume concentrates on grounds which once hosted League football but do so no longer, either because the club that played there no longer exists, has lost League status or, an increasingly common occurrence these days, has moved to a more modern ground that better suits its needs.**

The comfort and safety of spectators shot to the top of the table, so to speak, after the twin horrors of Bradford (1985) and Hillsborough (1989), when all-seater stadia became mandatory for the higher divisions. The financial imperatives of the modern game also dictate clubs must increase their matchday revenue, and that means getting more fans through the gate into bigger, purpose-built arenas. It was this that motivated Arsenal and may yet persuade Liverpool and Everton to leave their traditional and much-loved homes in favour of larger stadia.

While many old League football grounds are now supermarkets or housing estates, it is important to remember that, in the past, these sites once played host to significant and memorable moments in British football history. Where leagues were won and lost, scenes of promotion and relegation, of joy and despair. They were places generations called home on a Saturday afternoon, where families came together to support the club they loved so dearly.

While some of these redeveloped sites pay homage to their former status as sporting battlegrounds with a sole remaining floodlight, or a plaque where the centre circle once stood, others bear no trace of the history that went before. In a world of concrete identikit stadia, traditional football grounds are fast becoming few and far between.

While the relentless march of progress cannot be halted, and new grounds are undeniably well-equipped, many fans believe a little of their club's heart and soul fails to survive such moves. And it's certainly a source of regret to fans of a certain age that the locations where they witnessed football history in the making are now DIY superstores, supermarkets or housing. That is why we are delighted to have incorporated fans' reminiscences into our book.

With the limited space at its disposal, Lost League Grounds does not claim to be exhaustive. But we hope that it will bring back memories for 'oldies' while educating younger fans as to where their club has, literally, come from to be where it is today. We also acknowledge the assistance of many clubs and their historians in our researches: a fuller list appears elsewhere.

So join us on a journey of nostalgia as we take a look at these unique pieces of history that represent what, to many, is football's golden era.

Michael and Drew Heatley
2010

The authors would like to thank all those who supplied memories: their names should accompany their stories. Thanks also to the following, who contributed on the pictorial side.

Peter Smith (Airdrie), Peter Hawkridge (Barrow), David Martin (Bolton), Kevin Haley (Bradford PA), Geoff Mitchell (Chesterfield), Stevie McAneney (Clydebank), Matt Hudson (Colchester), Carl Newell (Coventry), Jim Brown (Coventry), Richard Tearle (Darlington), Dennis Cook (East Fife), James K. Corstorphine (East Fife), Michael White (Falkirk), Arthur Lynch (Hamilton), Stuart Fuller (Dartford), Chris Williams (Oxford), Matt Banyard (Rushden & Diamonds), Doug Parker (Scunthorpe), Mik Henry (Scunthorpe), Danny Davies (Shrewsbury), Graham Hamilton (Stirling Albion), Ryan Murray (St Johnstone), Richard Copp (Swansea), Jonathan Wilsher (Swansea), Paul Chialton (Wigan), David McKnight (Wimbledon), Steve Woffenden (Workington), Les Evans (Wrexham), Geraint Parry (Wrexham), Mark Comer (York). Aerofilms Ltd supplied the Port Vale and Sunderland pictures.

Otherwise uncredited photographic contributions are from Ken Coton www.ken.coton.btinternet.co.uk (black and white and colour action shots) and Bob Lilliman (colour static shots). Without them this book could not have been produced.

CONTENTS

PEEL PARK – ACCRINGTON STANLEY

Name:
Peel Park

Highest attendance:
17,634, vs. Blackburn Rovers,
15 November 1954

First league match:
Accrington Stanley 4–0 Rochdale,
3 September 1921

Final league match:
Accrington Stanley 0–2 Rochdale,
24 February 1962

Memorable moment:
Accrington Stanley vs. Blackburn Rovers,
15 November 1954 (first floodlit game)

Current stadium:
Crown Ground

Peel Park was home to the first incarnation of Accrington Stanley from 1919 to 1966, when the club resigned from the Football League mid-season. A similar fate had befallen rivals Accrington FC in 1893, the club resigning from the League after relegation from the top flight. Stanley Villa then took the town's name to become Accrington Stanley.

It was a new stand for Peel Park that effectively sealed the club's financial demise. Stanley purchased the Main Stand from the Aldershot Military Tattoo in 1958, and the transportation and erection costs of the stand – in which viewing was virtually impossible from some angles – brought the total cost to nearly £20,000, more expensive than if the club had built one itself.

Ambitious ideas for the ground such as the aforementioned stand, which was not designed to be used for viewing football, and being the first club to experiment with floodlights at a cost of £4,000 in 1954, were a step too far for a team that never progressed from the Third Division.

Though Stanley's attempt at the first-ever floodlit game in British football drew a record crowd of 17,634 for a friendly against Blackburn Rovers in 1954, these were the glory days for Peel Park. (Highest league attendance came the following April, 15,598, vs. York City.) It would be just seven years before the club would resign from the League mid-season, with a historical quirk bringing Rochdale to Peel Park for Stanley's final home League game just over four decades since they arrived for their first.

Peel Park was left abandoned and dilapidated upon Stanley's demise, and is now used as the adjacent Peel Park Primary School's playing fields. The Accrington Stanley that achieved promotion to the Football League in 2006 was founded in 1968 and plays at the Crown Ground, built that year and since expanded to 5,000 capacity.

MEMORIES

I remember a few things from the Peel Park days. I can always visualise how many cars where parked on streets like Manor St, Lodge St when Stanley were at home. This was the 1950s, not many people had cars then.

I also remember the all-Scottish Stanley team, George Stewart's goals in particular. Goalkeeper Tommy McQueen talking to the crowd behind the Coppice goal comes to mind.

One of the games I remember quite well was the cup match against Preston who were then, I think I'm right in saying, in the old first division. Stanley drew away at Preston, which was a great result, but lost the replay at Peel Park. There was a big crowd on that night.
Bernard Dawson

Accrington Stanley was one of the first clubs in the Football League to get lights, before Rovers and Burnley. If I remember rightly they were on eight telegraph poles, four on each side of the ground.
Jaysay

Of the players I saw pre-1960, John Ryden, a young Scottish centre half, stands out. He was a class above the rest – not surprising that he was snapped up by Spurs. Les Cocker was past his best when playing for us, but his class was apparent.

It was possible to watch the game from outside the ground when standing on the slope of the Coppice a bit higher up than the Peel Park pub.
Bob Dobson

BROOMFIELD PARK – AIRDRIEONIANS FC

Name:
Broomfield Park
Highest attendance:
24,000, vs. Hearts,
8 March 1952
First league match:
Airdrieonians 4–2 Port Glasgow Athletic,
25 August 1894
Final league match:
Airdrieonians 1–0 Dunfermline,
7 May 1994
Memorable moment:
Airdrieonians 11–1 Falkirk,
28 April 1951
Current stadium:
The Excelsior Stadium (Airdrie United)

Vacated by Airdrieonians in 1994 after a 102-year stay, Broomfield Park was an eccentric, claustrophobic and intimidating ground for any team in Scotland to visit. Airdrieonians FC missed out on a first ever promotion to the Scottish Premier League in 2002 before being wound up owing to debts even though on the cusp of success.

Broomfield was characterised by its imposing and quirky pavilion in the corner of the ground, its red diamond façade a feature that would be out of place in the era of the modern purpose-built stadium. Behind both goals were two uncovered curved terraces, with two covered stands running parallel up the length of the pitch. Four floodlight pylons sat atop the roofs of these.

Airdrieonians signed off at Broomfield in 1994, after a final-game victory over Dunfermline, with an uncertain future. They sold Broomfield to supermarket chain Safeway but, having not yet secured planning permission for a new stadium, they were forced to share with Clyde before finally moving to the 10,000-seater Excelsior Stadium in 1998 – titled after the team's original name upon their formation in 1878. But the team's stay there didn't last long as they went into liquidation with debts of over £3 million four years later, just a decade after finishing seventh in the Scottish Football League's Premier Division (the top flight before the Premier League was formed).

MEMORIES

The pie stand used to be located at the back of the stand near the fence separating the home and away fans. Someone had gone for the pies and Bovril early and was walking down the passageway between the Airdrie fans and the fence when the Diamonds scored. Naturally all the Airdrie fans ran to the fence to berate the opposition. When the crowd pulled back the guy's tray of pies and drinks were thrown all over him and he was cursing and swearing at the crowd – very funny at the time.
Diamonds1924

The Sun used to run a feature every week asking a player certain questions, one being – What's your least favourite ground? Quite often Broomfield was the least favourite ground owing to its intimidating atmosphere and the fact the fans were almost on top of the pitch. Dave Bowman and Duncan Ferguson of Dundee Utd used to get a really hard time there – especially 'Beast' Bowman.

To me Broomfield was a big part of why I supported Airdrie. It had a bad reputation and a volatile crowd, which as a young lad looking for a bit of excitement was right up my street. One on side you had the famous centre stand – old men famed for things like taking their batteries out their hearing aids and throwing them at opposing managers below. Other side, at the segregation fence you had the Section-B, and to round matters off as the players and officials left the pitch at the end into the famous pavilion, you usually had a few hundred fans gathered to hurl abuse, coins and anything else going at the opposing players and officials coming off. Can even remember Davie Kirkwood of Airdrie getting punched once coming off as Forfar had beaten us at home. Just punishment for a shocking defeat, ha ha!
OlderB

HIGHBURY - ARSENAL FC

Name:
Arsenal Stadium

Highest attendance:
73,295, vs. Sunderland,
9 March 1935

First league match:
Arsenal 2–1 Leicester Fosse,
6 September 1913

Final league match:
Arsenal 4–2 Wigan Athletic,
7 May 2006

Memorable moment:
Arsenal 2–0 Newcastle United,
16 May 1998
(Arsenal win the FA Premier League title)

Current stadium:
The Emirates Stadium

Built just before World War I when Arsenal moved north of the river from Woolwich, and vacated in 2006, Highbury is one of the most recent League stadiums to be replaced by a bigger and better model, and from 1919 onwards hosted only top-flight football. The first incarnation was designed by famed architect Archibald Leitch, well known for his association with British football stadiums, and was funded by then Arsenal chairman Sir Henry Norris.

Highbury (officially titled the Arsenal Stadium) opened towards the end of 1913 with a match against Leicester Fosse. Despite the ground being unfinished, it still attracted attention amongst the football elite and just seven years later was regularly hosting England internationals, as well as becoming an FA Cup semi-final venue.

The club bought out the lease to the ground midway through the 1920s and this allowed Highbury to be expanded and tailored to the Gunners' needs. The North Bank terrace was enlarged before the West Stand was completed in 1932 featuring a then state-of-the-art two-tiered design that housed 21,000 spectators.

Shortly after this the East Stand was erected. The focal point of Highbury, with its imposing façade and famed marble halls, it could seat 8,000 fans and was more than twice as expensive as the West Stand built four years previously.

The famous Highbury clock was originally at the back of the North Bank until it was covered; it was relocated to the South Stand, thenceforth known as the Clock End, in 1935. The switch was timely as the North Stand's roof lasted less than a decade, destroyed by bombing during World War II. Highbury was largely left alone until the 1990s, save for post-war repairs.

Post-Taylor Report adaptations saw a totally restructured North Bank open in 1993, seating 12,000 fans in two tiers and featuring a cantilevered roof. With Highbury now an all-seater stadium, the capacity was capped at slightly over 38,000 – around half that of rivals Manchester United. The call for more revenue through gate receipts and corporate opportunity saw Arsenal depart Highbury for the 60,000-capacity Emirates Stadium in 2006. Highbury has since been converted into apartments, with only the listed East and West Stands remaining.

MEMORIES

It was love at first sight… as a wide-eyed six year-old in 1979 I was completely blown away by the size, atmosphere and sense of history around Highbury, and despite witnessing a 1–0 defeat to Wolves I was hooked and wanted more.

Highbury made Arsenal special, the art deco grandeur of the East and West stands, the Clock End, just everything about it was special to me; if truth be told, for me football and Arsenal has never been the same since we left Highbury.
Adam Velasco

HOLKER STREET - BARROW

Name:
Holker Street

Highest attendance:
16,874, vs. Swansea City,
9 January 1954

First league match:
Barrow 0–2 Stockport County,
27 August 1921

Final league match:
Barrow 0–3 Brentford,
24 April 1972

Memorable moment:
Barrow 3–2 Crewe Alexandra,
24 April 1967
(en route to promotion from Fourth Division)

Current stadium:
Holker Street

Cumbria-based Barrow AFC moved to a former rubbish tip in Holker Street in 1909 after eight years playing at the Strawberry Ground and, later, Ainslie Street, and have remained there ever since. The club and ground played host to League football for 51 years before an on-field slump at the beginning of the 1970s.

By 1920 the stadium was enlarged to hold 20,000 fans after Barrow purchased the ground. Concrete terracing surrounded the pitch, and the South Stand was dismantled and moved to the west end, then known as the Steelworks End, with a larger stand built in its place.

Thirty years later the Holker Street End was covered and its opposite counterpart replaced, providing shelter on all four sides. Buying second-hand floodlights in 1963 was as close as Barrow got to the big time during their League stay; the club was voted out of the Football League in 1972, but still plays at Holker.

Now the Holker Street End is an uncovered terrace, and the Main Stand on the north side is situated on the halfway line with 'Barrow' picked out across the seats. The club offices are situated on the Crossbar – formerly Steelworks – End, the area reserved for away supporters. The South Stand is terracing with cover in the middle section.

After dropping down the non-League pyramid, a return to the Conference National has brought renewed hope that Holker Street could once again host League football in the not too distant future.

MEMORIES

As regards anecdotes, someone will probably sooner or later mention the winning goal against Plymouth on 9 November 1968, which was inadvertently 'scored' by the referee, Ivan Robinson. It is alleged to be a unique event in the Football League.

What about some of the ties in the FA Trophy runs in the early 1990s? The evening game when more than 5,000 turned up unexpectedly, so that the kick-off was significantly delayed. Or the semi-finals against the (now defunct, and always controversially spelt) 'Colne Dynamos'. The crowds outside the town hall after the final at Wembley…Some time later I recall

there was another trophy game against Dover – however, I can't really comment any further, since I was one of the hundreds (if not thousands) who were locked out of the ground, after the capacity had been reduced.

Quirky features? The racetrack – often said to have contributed significantly to the loss of Football League status? (It was a bit before my time.) And later the squash courts – in what is now the Crossbar and changing rooms. The frequent strong and cold winds driving in from the coast, which didn't help either the spectators or the players. The self-styled 'last streaker of the millennium', who made a very brief appearance running across the field in a game against Winsford on 30 December 1999 (reported in the local press). The Stephen Vaughan era, followed by the long struggle to save the club? The FA Cup tie against Bristol Rovers in November 2006 – a brave fight back to lose 2–3, after being 0–3 down (certain other notorious incidents featured on TV probably now best forgotten).

Spectator

BURNDEN PARK – BOLTON WANDERERS

Name:
Burnden Park
Highest attendance:
69,912, vs. Manchester City,
18 February 1933
First league match:
Bolton 3-1 Everton,
14 September 1895
Final league match:
Bolton 4–1 Charlton Athletic,
25 April 1997
Memorable moment:
Tottenham Hotspur 3–1 Sheffield United,
27 April 1901 (FA Cup final replay)
Current stadium:
Reebok Stadium

Prior to its demolition in 1999, Burnden Park was home to Bolton Wanderers for over 100 years. From the halcyon days of the 1930s through to the 1960s, to the leaner periods of lower-division football, the stadium saw it all.

After a period of 'wandering' around different grounds, and a 15-year residency at Pike's Lane, Preston North End were the first visitors to Burnden Park in 1895 in a friendly. Just six years later the stadium would play host to an FA Cup final replay between Tottenham Hotspur and Sheffield United.

If that was a high point, the low point in the history of both club and ground would definitely be the 'Burnden Park Disaster' in which 33 spectators were killed owing to overcrowding. Over 65,000 fans crammed into the stadium to witness Bolton play Stanley Matthews's Stoke in an FA Cup quarter-final in March 1946, but, as the game kicked off, tragedy struck, with scenes that would become all too familiar just over 40 years later at Hillsborough.

The 1980s and early 90s saw a lull at Burnden Park; Bolton were playing Second and Third Division football and attendances that once topped 60,000 now barely reached 20,000, due in no small part to a section of the embankment being sold to a supermarket chain. But an upwardly mobile club such as Bolton would not languish for long, and the realisation of their ambitions required a stadium to match.

Bolton's last season at Burnden Park was arguably their most successful. They were promoted to the Premier League as champions in 1997 and welcomed Charlton for their last game before moving to the purpose-built 28,000-capacity Reebok Stadium, running out comfortable 4–1 winners. The ground was demolished two years later and an Asda supermarket now stands on the site.

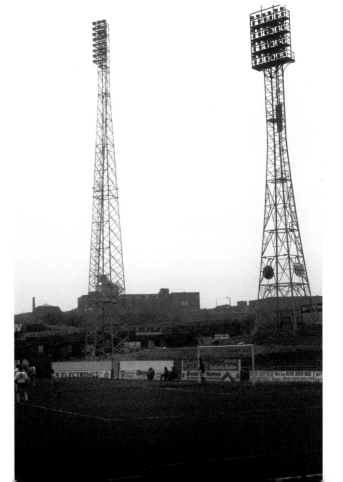

MEMORIES

Two stick out miles for me...

1. During the second leg of the playoff semi-final in May 1995 versus Wolves hugging and kissing the stranger next to me as Super John McGinlay scored the second of his two goals that night in extra time to secure a place at Wembley in a 3–2 aggregate win. And he should never have been on the pitch at all, having floored a Wolves player (David Kelly I believe) with a couple of haymakers under the nose of the ref when the score was still 0–0.

2. FA Cup tie versus the supposedly lowly Chesterfield in 1997. Chesterfield turned us over 0–3 with some unknown whippersnapper getting a hat-trick. In usual Bolton style we didn't take advantage and sign the kid there and then, instead letting him spend the next six years bouncing between Southampton and Blackburn. We did get our man in the end, though, signing Kevin Davies in 2003.

David Martin

YORK STREET – BOSTON UNITED

Name:
York Street

Highest attendance:
11,000, vs. Derby County,
9 January 1974

First league match:
Boston United 2–2 Bournemouth,
10 August 2002

Final league match:
Boston United 1–1 Torquay United,
28 April 2007

Memorable moment:
Boston United 2–0 Lincoln City,
24 August 2002 (Boston's first ever League victory)

Current stadium:
York Street

An unmistakably British-sounding stadium for a team that sounds as if it's from across the Atlantic, York Street has housed Boston United since 1933, though former club custodians insisted the site has been in use by various Boston teams since the 1800s.

The stadium has endured a number of name changes throughout the years; prior to United's formation it was known as Main Ridge, changing to Shodfriars Lane before becoming York Street. In 2009 it succumbed to taking the name of a sponsor, becoming the Jakemans Stadium.

The Main Stand runs the length of the pitch on the north side, and is named the Staffsmart Stand, again for sponsorship reasons. Opposite is the Spayne Road Terrace, a covered terrace generally considered the most atmospheric.

Behind the west goal is the Town End Terrace. Formerly for away fans, it was revered so much by Boston fans that they forced travelling supporters to a section of the York Street Stand, the oldest stand in the ground, opposite the other goal on the east side.

Boston's brief five-year stay in the League was not without incident, York Street becoming the stamping ground of a former England great and football legend in Paul Gascoigne. Though Gazza only played five games for the club, he still evoked a positive response from the York Street faithful.

The Pilgrims' tenure in the Football League ended in 2007 when the team was relegated and unceremoniously dropped a further two divisions for entering administration. Yet although the club's former chairman may have fled like the original Pilgrim Fathers 400 years before, Boston United and their York Street home remain, both harbouring the hope of League football once more.

MEMORIES

My first memory (although by no means the first match I attended, so my parents tell me) was the defeat of Bromsgrove Rovers in January 1967. I was probably the only person standing on the slag heap now known as the Town End when Ken Oxford let a weak shot get straight through his legs in the first few minutes. United went on to win 9–1.
David Whittle, Supporters Direct Liaison, BUFC Supporters Trust.

When Paul Gascoigne joined lowly Boston United, one of the club's directors likened his arrival to a visit from the Pope. It was pandemonium, he claimed, as Pilgrims flocked to catch a glimpse of the town's most famous inhabitant since Lord Archer left North Sea Camp prison.

The reaction was exactly what the new owners of the League Two club were hoping for when they recruited the hero of Italia '90, and the prospect of Gascoigne's debut put 33 per cent on their opening-day gate.

A Boston glee party was promised but, like most things in the 37-year-old's roller-coaster life, the rest of the story has not quite unfolded as planned. Gascoigne missed that first game owing to a stomach ulcer and it was another three weeks before the new player-coach made his York Street bow.

By then 'Gazzamania' had subsided and a crowd of just 2,698 witnessed Boston's 3–1 win over Chester. The attendance was even lower for Saturday's 2–2 draw with Shrewsbury, while tickets for tonight's Carling Cup clash against Fulham – the most high-profile game in the club's history – are still available.
The Evening Standard, September 2004

PARK AVENUE – BRADFORD PARK AVENUE

Name:
Park Avenue

Highest attendance:
34,429, vs. Leeds United,
25 December 1931

First league match:
Bradford Park Avenue 1–0 Hull City,
1 September 1908

Final league match:
Bradford Park Avenue 0–5 Scunthorpe United,
4 April 1970

Memorable moment:
Bradford Park Avenue 2–2 Birmingham City,
2 March 1946 (FA Cup quarter-final)

Current stadium:
Horsfall Stadium

Park Avenue was so special to its inhabitants that they adopted its name – Bradford Park Avenue played League football at the ground for 62 years, 1908–1970. But even the sale of the ground three years later could not stop the club from going to the wall in 1974.

Despite being newly formed, Bradford signalled their intentions by commissioning Archibald Leitch to design their home, which sat adjacent to Bradford Park Avenue cricket ground. Upon completion it could accommodate 37,000 and was considered superior to more successful neighbours City's Valley Parade.

The ground had three covered stands, one of which was pitchside and seated spectators. It had an impressive gabled roof and ran up to the ground's most distinctive feature, a pavilion known as the 'Dolls House'; this was similar to the cottage at Fulham, and was situated in the corner of the ground next to the goal-side uncovered terracing.

Top-flight football was achieved at Park Avenue fairly quickly, just seven years after the football club's formation. An opening-day 2–1 home defeat to champions Blackburn Rovers would not set the tone for a season, in which Park Avenue finished in ninth place, just five points behind table-toppers Everton.

Upon selling their home in 1973 Park Avenue fell into disrepair, with the stands demolished. And while a Sunday League incarnation of Park Avenue returned to play a fixture there in 1987, an indoor cricket centre was eventually erected on part of the pitch, signalling the end.

The quiet neighbour had taken over. The re-formed Bradford Park Avenue now play at the 5,000-capacity Horsfall Stadium.

MEMORIES

Although it was almost 45 years ago I can remember clearly the first time I ever went to the Park Avenue football ground. The occasion was a mid-table Fourth Division clash with Chesterfield in early 1966. As well as being my first ever football match the occasion was even more special because the match was played under floodlights.

I went to the match with my brother and I can remember us walking along the balcony that ran behind the main stand and faced onto the cricket field. After walking slowly in near darkness behind a queue of people we climbed up a few stairs and went through some wooden doors and suddenly we were in the brightness of the football stadium; it was like stepping into Wonderland.

The very first thing I saw was the players warming up on the pitch. Bradford played in all white in those days and the kit seemed to almost glow in the floodlights. We sat in the Canterbury Avenue End stand which, being elevated some 20 feet or more, had a fantastic view of the pitch. The bulk of the noise though came from the Horton End, which was behind the goal to my left. Avenue won 3–0 and I was hooked for life.
Kevin Haley

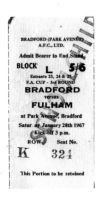

GOLDSTONE GROUND – BRIGHTON & HOVE ALBION

Name:
Goldstone Ground

Highest attendance:
36,747, vs. Fulham,
27 December 1958

First league match:
Brighton & Hove Albion 0–0 Merthyr Town,
1 September 1920

Final league match:
Brighton & Hove Albion 1–0 Doncaster Rovers,
26 April 1997

Memorable moment:
Brighton A–A York City,
27 April 1996 (abandoned owing to protest over vacation of the Goldstone Ground)

Current stadium:
Withdean Stadium

Brighton's recent history is characterised by the club's lack of a permanent home since they vacated the Goldstone Ground in 1997 after a near 100-year residency.

The vast expanse of terracing on the Goldstone's East Stand had a natural slant that ran parallel to Goldstone Lane behind it, while the West Stand opposite extended along only three-quarters of the touchline. A temporary stand was erected in 1979 to fill the remaining gap and held approximately 1,000, but was dismantled six years later.

The original South Stand behind the goal was built after Brighton first became tenants, moving from Hove cricket ground in 1904, but was renovated after the First World War and completely rebuilt on new foundations in 1954. It became an all-seated stand in 1980 after being heavily damaged by fire. The opposing North Stand was opened in 1931 and became fully covered in 1958, though roofing was temporarily removed in the late 1970s. 1961 saw the installation of floodlights.

The Goldstone saw First Division football for three seasons between 1979 and 1983 and played host to some FA Cup triumphs on the way to Brighton's first and only Cup final appearance, including a 4–0 demolition of Manchester City and quarter-final victory over Norwich City.

After selling the Goldstone to developers without consulting the fans, then-chairman Bill Archer endured over a year's worth of protests, the boiling point being reached at the game against York City in 1996, abandoned after a pitch invasion; Brighton were granted a temporary stay of execution, but a year later they were forced to leave, the final game at the Goldstone having the added importance of being crucial to League survival. They beat Doncaster Rovers 1–0 to set up a relegation decider against Hereford on the final day, which ended a 1–1 draw, sending the Bulls down on goals scored.

The Goldstone is now a retail outlet park, while Brighton, having lodged with Gillingham in 1997–99 and the Withdean, plan to open their purpose-built ground at Falmer in 2011.

MEMORIES

The Goldstone was one of those grounds from a bygone era. I stood on the North Stand with my dad and my brother from the age of seven until the ground was closed in 1997. The sight lines weren't great, the east side of the ground was virtually closed and the capacity had been slashed several times over its final years but, when it counted, the atmosphere was electric and we loved the place.

The so-called 'twelfth man' effect of a decent atmosphere/crowd was never more evident than the final season when Brighton pulled off a great escape and avoided relegation to the Football Conference. With no stadium for the following season at that point and staring the Conference in the face the club was on the brink. As the season drew to a close and the team guided by Steve Gritt turned things around the crowd willed the Albion on and the electric atmosphere seemed to lift the team when they needed it most, peaking with the 1–0 final home match win.

Whether that amount of passion and atmosphere can be replicated at the new Falmer remains to be seen but for those there on that last day at the Goldstone I'm sure that feeling of elation created by thousands of Albion supporters crammed into the crumbling old place will never be forgotten.
Nick Westcott

In September 1993, Brighton played Manchester Utd in the second round of the League Cup, and about 30 seconds before we equalised the Goldstone crowd witnessed a young lad called David Beckham, who made his first ever appearance in professional football as a substitute. In the video footage of the moment you can clearly hear many of the 14,000 or so chanting 'Who the hell are you?' at Fergie's latest fledgling!

The Goldstone under floodlights was an incredibly atmospheric venue and the acoustics from the North Stand made even the smallest crowd seem rather loud. It is sadly missed by all Albion fans who ever saw us play there.
Aaron Berry

EASTVILLE STADIUM – BRISTOL ROVERS

Name:
Eastville Stadium

Highest attendance:
38,472, vs. Preston North End,
30 January 1960

First league match:
Bristol Rovers 3–2 Newport County,
1 September 1920

Final league match:
Bristol Rovers 1–1 Chesterfield,
26 April 1986

Memorable moment:
Bristol Rovers 7–0 Brighton & Hove Albion,
29 November 1952 (record home victory en route to Third Division South title)

Current stadium:
Memorial Stadium

Eastville Stadium's close proximity to the Stapleton Gasworks gave Bristol Rovers fans the nickname 'Gasheads'. Their time there had its explosive moments, but over the years it became clear the location was far from satisfactory for a football stadium. Hosting League football for 66 years between 1920 and 1986, Eastville saw Rovers win over half their 1,279 games in front of their loyal fans, before financial difficulties forced them to move out.

The hub of activity for the die-hard Rovers fans was the curved Stapleton Road End, behind which was the aforementioned gasworks. The large covered terrace was known as the Tote End owing to displaying the betting totaliser for the greyhound racing that also occurred in the stadium, and would have a large effect on the club's history. The totaliser would be replaced by advertising in 1982.

The inactivity in the wartime period affected a lot of clubs financially, and Bristol Rovers was no exception. The ground was sold to the Bristol Greyhound Racing Association, and Rovers were granted a lease on 8 March 1940 at £400 per year to continue playing on the ground for a further 21 years. Further financial assistance saw the club come under the company's control briefly in 1945.

The racing of dogs was not the only other sport to be hosted at Eastville. It hosted a wide variety of events over the following years, including the addition of speedway in the 1970s and even a Sunday market. That, coupled with the building of the M32 motorway, which encroached on the stadium, meant it was only a matter of time before Rovers had to find a new home, but money was not readily available.

In August 1980 a fire gutted the South Stand, destroying the club's offices and changing rooms and, with the ground being described as a shell, Rovers temporarily moved to Bath City's Twerton Park in 1986. The move saved the club an annual cost of £30,000 plus expenses, but the historic decision to leave the club's spiritual home was regretted by many.

Greyhound racing continued in their absence, but the stadium was shut down permanently in 1997. In 1999 an Ikea superstore was erected on the site, retaining a solitary floodlight as a tribute to the old stadium. Rovers returned to Bristol in 1996, taking up residence at Bristol Rugby Club's 12,000-capacity Memorial Stadium and eventually buying the freehold.

MEMORIES

Late in the game, with us one down, the ball went into the rosebushes behind our goal at the Tote End. The ball boys went to get it, but kept backing off because of the thorns. The crowd were getting angry with them and starting to shout. Dick Sheppard realised what was going on and ran into the middle of the bushes, completely ignoring them in his shorts, to get the ball back!
Larry Lloyd's a Giant

ABBEY STADIUM – CAMBRIDGE UNITED

Name:
Abbey Stadium
Highest attendance:
14,000, vs. Chelsea,
1 May 1970
First league match:
Cambridge United 1–1 Lincoln City,
15 August 1970
Final league match:
Cambridge United 0–0 Notts County,
7 May 2005
Memorable moment:
Cambridge United 2–0 Swansea City,
11 May 1991 (United win the Third Division title by one point)
Current stadium:
Abbey Stadium

Abbey Stadium was home to Cambridge United when they attained League status from 1970 and remained so until the club's relegation to the Conference in 2005. During this time it played host to many an FA Cup moment, and saw United narrowly miss out on becoming founder members of the FA Premier League in 1992. The resulting slump saw them and their stadium lose their League status in 2005.

Then known as Abbey United, Cambridge moved to the site in 1932 after failing to settle in various venues around the city, including a common and the nearby Station Farm, known affectionately as 'Celery Trenches'. The land was donated by then-president Henry Clement. The team played without a grandstand for two years before work was completed in 1934.

In the 1950s United fans helped construct terracing on the South and West Stands, but as the club prepared to campaign for League admittance in the mid-1960s the latter was renovated and became a covered grandstand; the east side was also covered and renamed the Habbin Stand, after a former supporters' club president. The grandstand was extended to the full length of the pitch in 1980, and from then the ground was largely unaltered.

Financial problems have dogged the club for years, resulting in the club selling the ground to an outside company in 2004. In recent years a series of sponsorship deals have seen the stands and the stadium itself renamed to advertise the companies bankrolling them. The stadium is officially known as the R Costings Abbey Stadium, with the Marston's Smooth South Stand behind the goal, which opened in 2002, emblazoned with CUFC on black and orange seats under a cantilevered roof.

United have twice missed out on a League return by the narrowest of margins in recent years, finishing second in both the 2007–08 and 2008–09 seasons and failing at the final hurdle. How different things could have been had they won the playoffs in 1992…

MEMORIES

Abbey Stadium saw Sunday service of the highest order yesterday as Cambridge United continued their advance up the Second Division table with a dazzling dismissal of Leicester City.

The win, which leaves them in third place, exorcised the memory of their midweek defeat by Manchester United and provided further confirmation that their much-vaunted striker Dion Dublin is destined for the higher echelon even if the club is not.

Dublin was substituted at Old Trafford and consigned to the reserves on Thursday after what his manager John Beck described as a 'below-par performance'; but there were no complaints yesterday. The gangling 22-year-old scored twice against his hometown team and was given a standing ovation when he came off in the 75th minute.
The Guardian, September 1991

The Abbey Stadium is not one of the cathedrals of the English game. Rather, it is a collection of garden sheds surrounding a green and pleasant pitch upon which the ball rarely lands.
Mail on Sunday, March 1992

In a quiet corner of Cambridge where the only students are lost students, lies the compact Abbey Stadium. Most people agree that a new ground is required, preferably one with a car park, but in the city of the tow-away scheme this looks about as likely as a compliment on the U's style of play from a national newspaper.
The Independent, August 1992

NINIAN PARK – CARDIFF CITY

Name:

Ninian Park

Highest attendance:

57,800, vs. Arsenal,

22 April 1953

First league match:

Cardiff City 0–0 Clapton Orient,

30 August 1920

Final league match:

Cardiff City 0–3 Ipswich Town,

25 April 2009

Memorable moment:

Cardiff City 1–0 Real Madrid,

10 March 1971

(European Cup Winners' Cup quarter-final)

Current stadium:

Cardiff City Stadium

Ninian Park's history was cut short one year shy of its century when Cardiff moved into their brand new Cardiff City Stadium in 2009, but the ground that was built on the site of a rubbish tip is synonymous with many a generation's memories of the Bluebirds. Having arrived from the nearby Sophia Gardens, newly professional Cardiff named the ground in honour of Lord Ninian Crichton-Stuart, who helped secure the lease.

Upon election to the Football League in 1920 the Canton Stand was erected (later to be known as the Spar Family Stand). Covered and with some seating, it was situated at the north goal end. Eight years later saw the opposite Grangetown End covered. Ninian Park's modest wooden Main Stand was destroyed by fire in 1937, and was replaced by a larger, more imposing structure. Opposite the Grandstand running along the touchline on the east side of the ground is the Popular Bank, referred to as the Bob Bank. This stand was particularly deep and had 'Cardiff' imprinted on the seats.

Floodlights were installed in 1960 and it was to prove a timely innovation as Ninian Park saw a number of European ties in the 1960s and '70s, with Cardiff qualifying for the European Cup Winners Cup by winning the Welsh Cup on a number of occasions. The most notable tie without doubt was a memorable 1–0 victory over Spanish champions Real Madrid in the quarter-finals in 1971.

The Grangetown End's roof was demolished in 1977 in compliance with the Safety at Sports Grounds Act, only to be rebuilt in 2001, and the following year saw the installation of a plasma screen. Cardiff's farewell to Ninian Park was one of heartbreak when they lost 3–0 to Ipswich Town, which, coupled with a final-day loss away to Sheffield Wednesday, caused them to miss out on a playoff spot on goals scored thanks to Preston North End's victory against Queens Park Rangers.

MEMORIES

As a 13-year-old on Friday 15th April 1960 I was told by a friend in my class at Mill St School, Pontypridd, that we were going to watch Cardiff City tomorrow, playing some team called Aston or something like that. Now he was the kind of friend you just did not say no to; even though I had no inclination to go, I was too timid to say no.

Saturday duly arrived and I conned 2s 6d (about 12 pence) from my mother, who thought I had gone barking mad.

Ponty Station, steam trains galore; I was in my element but still trying to think of a way out of going to this bloody football match – no chance with my mate in charge of the situation.

Ninian Park Halt, crowds milling the roads like ants, smells I had never experienced before from various vendors. This was turning into an great adventure, but I had to go to this damn footy match; I could have quite happily parked myself at Ninian Park Halt and watched the steam trains all afternoon, but I dared not mention it or I could have been in mighty big trouble on Monday.

We ambled down to the Grange turnstile, which relieved us

of 6d (about 2.5 pence) I think, and proceeded to the front of the junior section (to the right of the Grange goal as you look towards the pitch) where I was in effect pinned to the wall at the front for the next two hours. I often think of this, particularly since Hillsborough.

Oh how I wished I were on Ponty common playing Cowboys and Indians with my 'proper friends'. What to do? A pasty from someone patrolling the perimeter of the pitch was divine and a little later a hot drink (can't remember what) from someone else on patrol with what looked like a rocket pack on his back, which was in fact a drinks dispenser. The players duly appeared to a loud roar as I was trying to fathom why they had the alphabet all along the Bob Bank wall facing the pitch, and what was that little cabin on stilts between the Grange and Enclosure (lower grandstand)? Was it the sheriff's office?

Players kept running here, there and everywhere, my eyes looking here there and everywhere except the play and then an explosion of sound as City scored and I was scared. The joy and elation on people's faces, I could not move so I screamed and shouted like everyone else. God knows what I said. Strangely my eyes stopped wandering and became fixated on the play. I needed another goal, I needed to be scared again, to get my wee heart pounding nineteen to the dozen; it was not to be that day, I did not want to leave at the end, people saying we have been promoted to Division One – what the hell is promotion and what the hell is a Division?

Found out a bit about promotion over the past 50 years and one hell of a lot more about relegation. My heart still goes nineteen to the dozen but I do not get frightened too often now, Millennium Stadium excepted; I hope a bit of fright may creep into my make-up as we reach the business end of this 2009–10 season.

So as a boy and a man I have the most wonderful memories of Ninian. My mate who bullied me to go 50 years ago? Never been since, bully for him!

William Tromans (known as Tony)

SEALAND ROAD & DEVA STADIUM – CHESTER CITY

Name:

Sealand Road & Deva Stadium

Highest attendance:

20,500, vs. Chelsea, 16 January 1952 (Sealand Road)

5,987, vs. Scarborough, 17 April 2004 (Deva Stadium)

First league match:

Chester City 3–1 Halifax,

12 September 1931 (Sealand Road)

Chester City 3–0 Burnley,

5 September 1992 (Deva Stadium)

Final league match:

Chester City 2–0 Rotherham United,

28 April 1990 (Sealand Road)

Chester City 1–2 Darlington,

2 May 2009 (Deva Stadium)

Memorable moment:

Chester City 2–2 Aston Villa, 15 January 1975

(League Cup semi-final) (Sealand Road)

Chester City 3–1 Hereford United,

23 April 1994 (en route to promotion from the Third

Division) (Deva Stadium)

Current stadium:

Deva Stadium

Chester has the distinction of having two former League grounds in Sealand Road and the Deva Stadium; one lost its status through demolition, the other through the club's relegation. Chester FC (they added the City in 1983) moved to the former in 1906 from Whipcord Lane and were elected to the League in 1931. Behind the goals were the Sealand Road End, and the commonly named Kop. A new main stand was built in 1979, but as it was built behind the existing stand, there is a large gap between it and the pitch, leading to criticism of its atmospheric effect.

City signed off at their home of over 80 years with a victory over Rotherham United that spared them saying farewell with relegation. Sealand Road was sold to property developers in 1990 owing to financial pressures, and was left derelict for three years while homeless Chester took up residence at Macclesfield Town's Moss Rose ground. The stadium was demolished in 1993 in favour of a retail park, by which point Chester had moved to the newly built Deva Stadium nearby.

Named after the Roman fort and settlement that eventually became Chester, the Deva Stadium held just over 5,000 supporters and was the first to comply with the Taylor Report, including spaces for disabled supporters and automatic turnstiles. It is a modest stadium that took just eight months to complete – and, interestingly enough, three-quarters of it is actually located in Wales, with only half of the East Stand, named the Vaughan East Stand for sponsorship reasons, located in England.

The aforementioned East, South and West Stands are seated, while there is terracing in the Harry McNally Terrace, named as such in 2006 after a former Chester manager. The Deva Stadium hasn't provided much luck in League football for Chester, as they were relegated to Division Three in their first season at the ground. They bounced back at the first attempt, but successive relegations in 1995 and 2000 saw them lose their League status. Despite making a brief return in 2004, Chester dropped back into the Conference in 2009, completing their lost League grounds brace. The club was wound up in March 2010 after succumbing to the combination of a 25-point deduction, breaches of Conference rules and financial problems.

MEMORIES

I was at Sealand Road to witness them destroy the remnants of the mighty Leeds United team of the 1970s 3–0. What a night that was – the veteran Chester centre-forward Derek Draper caused mayhem in the Leeds defence with his glancing headers, and the whole town went absolutely wild at the final whistle. The team then beat Blackpool 1–0 before we all travelled to St James' Park in Newcastle for a dreary 0–0 stalemate.

The following round was the semi-final where the Sealers, bidding to be the first fourth division team to get to Wembley, drew the formidable Aston Villa, whose ranks included the legendary goal scorer Ray Graydon. The first leg took place at Sealand Road and the town was in a state of near hysteria as the game approached.

I remember when I entered the little ground with my mates Steve Porter, Paul Manski and Ian Brown, it was filled to such capacity that we were picked up by this unseen force and carried two sections down from our ticket allocation. When the game ended it was the same – the crush was absolutely indescribable. We didn't need to walk anywhere – we were simply picked up by a wave of humanity and swept en masse down to the exit doors where the force squeezed us through the gates and poured us out stumbling into the street. It was very frightening and I shall never forget it.

The awful events at Hillsborough in 1989 were still 15 years away but something just as dreadful could easily have taken place that night in Sealand Road if a barrier had collapsed. As it was, once we were out we thought no more of the danger and the only talk in the bars that night was about the famous 2–2 draw we had all just witnessed.
Simon Catterall

SALTERGATE – CHESTERFIELD

Name:
The Recreation Ground (Saltergate)

Highest attendance:
30,561, vs. Tottenham Hotspur,
12 February 1938

First league match:
Chesterfield 2-2 Lincoln,
9 September 1899

Final league match:
Chesterfield 2-1 Bournemouth,
8 May 2010

Memorable moment:
Chesterfield 1-0 Wrexham,
9 March 1997 (FA Cup quarter-final)

Chesterfield could lay claim to being the first team to imaginatively title their home the Recreation Ground, as they were based there from 1871. Consequently regarded as one of the country's oldest football stadiums, it endured its time as a League venue with minimal change to its appearance. It is more popularly known, however, as Saltergate. The ground's record attendance listed was in the FA Cup; the Football League record of 28,268 came against Newcastle just over a decade later, but by the time of its closure the capacity had been reduced to 8,504.

Like most grounds of the time it was shared by the sports of football and cricket, but this double life ended shortly before Chesterfield's League debut at the end of the 19th century. 1921 saw the first alteration of the stadium when it had to move south by 20 feet to accommodate the extension of Cross Street behind it.

The Main Stand was constructed in 1936 and remained largely untouched for the remainder of its existence, while its opposite number, the Compton Street Terrace, had received just minor roof improvements and the installation of seating since its completion in 1921. The designer of the Main Stand was also responsible for the main stand at the Baseball Ground (Derby County's former ground) and they look almost identical. For this reason, and the ground's dilapidated state, it was used in the 2009 Brian Clough bio-pic The Damned United.

The Kop end was roofed in 1960 and it was another seven years before Chesterfield became the last League club to play a competitive match under floodlights. The stadium from then gradually began to look its age as the years passed, and in 2010 the club moved to the new 10,000seater B2net Stadium; the power to resist change proved even too hard for Chesterfield.

MEMORIES

This is a lovely football ground, but we've got nothing here. If you wanted a sandwich now I wouldn't know where to find you one. The new place will have everything. There will be some tears today, but we have to do it, for progress.
Barrie Hubbard

Chesterfield fans could not hold their emotions back in the closing seconds of the home game against Bournemouth, swarming on to the pitch from the Kop end after a low strike from the midfielder Derek Niven, five minutes into injury time, ensured that the club's 139-year tenure of its Saltergate ground would finish with a 2-1 victory.

Rusty, rickety Saltergate, one of the oldest football grounds in England and therefore the world, played on by Chesterfield since 1871, will now be demolished and houses built on the site. The club, formed in 1866, the Football League's fourth oldest, will forge its modern future in a £13m, 10,500 all-seater stadium, its name already sold for sponsorship to b2net, a data company.
The Guardian

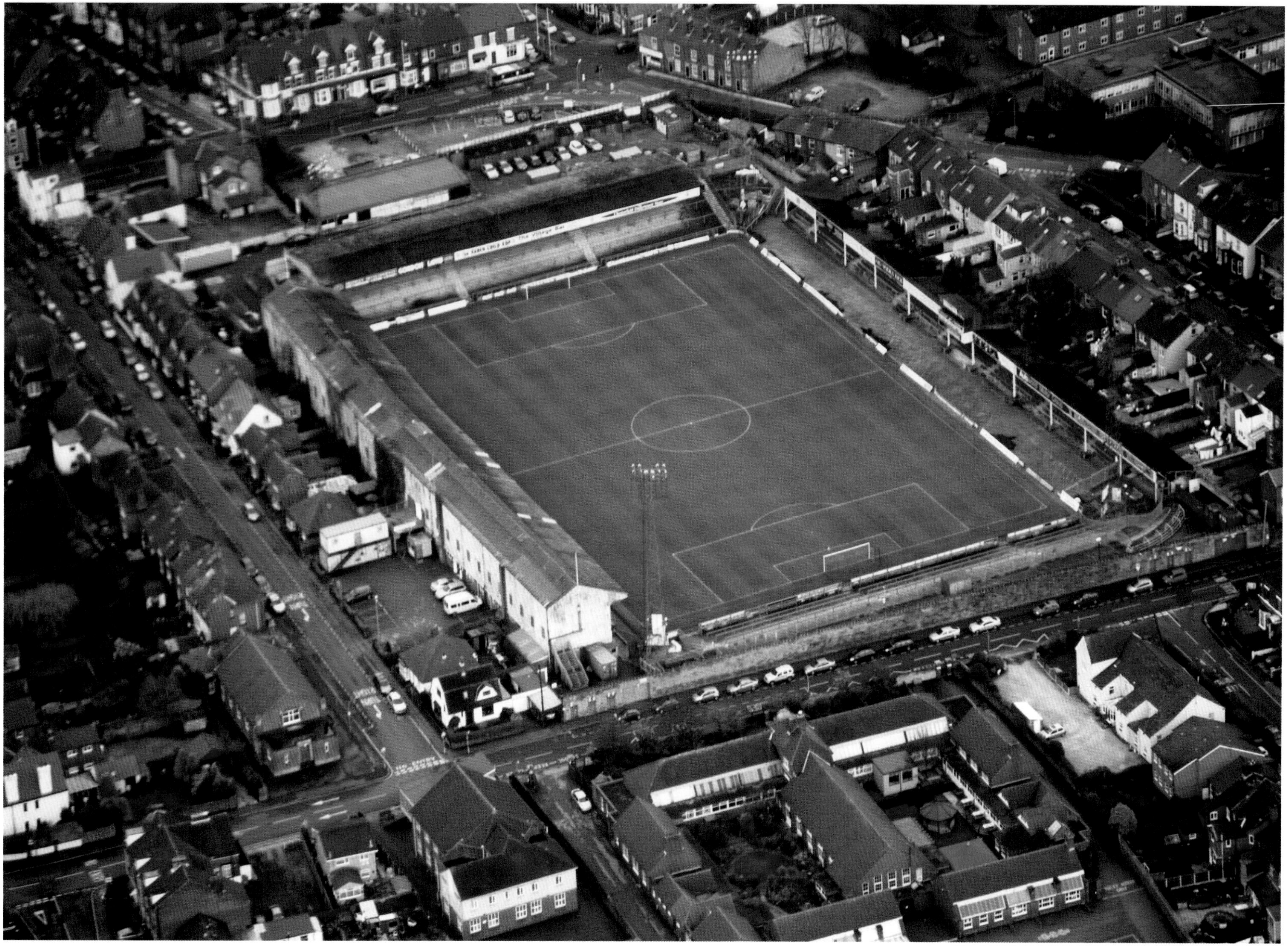

SHAWFIELD STADIUM – CLYDE

Name:
Shawfield Stadium

Highest attendance:
52,000, vs. Glasgow Rangers,
21 November 1908

First league match:
Clyde 0–0 Glasgow Celtic,
27 August 1898

Final league match:
Clyde 4–2 Alloa Athletic,
28 April 1986

Memorable moment:
Clyde 5–0 Falkirk,
5 March 1955
(Scottish Cup quarter-final)

Current stadium:
Broadwood Stadium

Scottish club Clyde FC moved to Shawfield Stadium in Rutherglen 21 years after forming on the banks of the River Clyde in 1898. Having previously played at Barrowfield Park, they had been admitted to the Scottish Football League in 1891 and their previous ground didn't have the facilities to accommodate League football. Upon their arrival at Shawfield in the summer, the race was on to create a stadium from a barren patch of land in a matter of months, in time for the new season.

By the time Clyde drew with neighbours Celtic in their first League game at Shawfield, the grandstand was essentially completed, with banking enclosing the pitch. This would last only 16 years, however, as a fire would destroy it, along with the club's entire archive of historical documents.

Shawfield was on the border of Glasgow and Lanarkshire, leaving Clyde with a crisis of identity. In the 1970s Glasgow was expanded to incorporate Rutherglen, before further change meant the town was classed as South Lanarkshire in its own right, though this was after Clyde had left the stadium.

In a move similar to Bristol Rovers, Clyde sold Shawfield to their greyhound-racing tenants in 1935, Shawfield taking on similar characteristics of Rovers' Eastville Stadium with a large betting totaliser behind the goal and racetrack around the pitch. The greyhound company's development plans would eventually oust Clyde in 1986 – in contrast to Rovers, who worked in tandem with their canine chums.

The 1950s saw many a cup victory en route to two Scottish Cup successes in 1955 and 1958, a highlight being a 5–0 hammering of Falkirk in the '55 semi-finals, though Clyde's success in the League was a mix of highs and lows, suffering seven relegations and consequent promotions at Shawfield.

Upon leaving Shawfield in 1986, Clyde shared with rivals Partick Thistle at Firhill for five years, before moving on to share Douglas Park with Hamilton Academical. Clyde returned to a home of their own after nearly a decade in the wilderness when they moved into the Broadwood Stadium in 1994. Situated in North Lanarkshire, it would be the third town in which the wandering Clyde would reside; hopes are high of stability in the future.

MEMORIES

Whereas Broadwood is largely indistinguishable from any other stadium built in recent years, Shawfield, where the greyhounds still run, is a monument to a long-forgotten era, all rickety grandstands, concrete terraces and crush barriers.

The playing surface was so far distant – across both speedway cinders and greyhound track – it was not unusual to spot spectators watching the game through binoculars.

As one-time Scotland coach Craig Brown, [former Clyde manager] recalls: 'When we were training on the pitch it wasn't unusual to hear a tannoy announcement informing us to pack up and go elsewhere – or words to that effect – because the greyhound time-trials were starting.

'They didn't want us hitting the dogs with a stray ball. To be fair, most of the greyhounds had cost a hell of a lot more than my players.'

The Telegraph, January 2006

KILBOWIE PARK – CLYDEBANK

Name:

Kilbowie Park

Highest attendance:

14,900, vs. Hibernian,

10 February 1965

First league match:

Clydebank 3–5 Albion Rovers,

8 October 1966

Final league match:

Clydebank 1–3 Hamilton Academical,

27 April 1996

Memorable moment:

Clydebank 2–1 St Johnstone,

4 May 1985

(en route to promotion to the Scottish Premier League)

Current stadium:

Holm Park

Kilbowie Park was home to Scottish side Clydebank, whose demise is bound up with the ground, as well as fellow team Airdrieonians, who folded in 2002. The football fans in Clydebank were no strangers to going out of business; four different incarnations bearing the name were in existence prior to the Clydebank that would inhabit Kilbowie Park in 1965.

Kilbowie was overlooked by buildings and largely uncovered, its floodlights towering over the low terracing. The club's offices, half stand and half office block, were actually situated behind the goal, giving a slightly strange appearance. At least the pen-pushers were close to the front line.

The ground has the distinction of being the first of the 'all-seater' stadiums; Clydebank installed benches running along the terracing in 1977 upon being promoted to the Scottish Premier League. Owing to the costs to comply with safety regulations for grounds with a capacity greater than 10,000, Clydebank found it cheaper to reduce the stadium's capacity to just under that amount, and therefore escape any substantial financial outlay.

But expenditure in football in never too far away and Clydebank were forced to sell the stadium by the club's owners and founders the Steedman Brothers, vacating after 30 years in 1996 with a new stadium in the offing. It never came to fruition. Ground sharing in the years to follow would not help the Bankies' financial situation and, in 2002, Jim Ballantyne bought the club to merge it with recently defunct Airdrieonians to form Airdrie United. Kilbowie Park was bought as the site of a retail park for just £600,000.

MEMORIES

I went to most Clydebank home games at Kilbowie between 1965 and 1973–74. All my family are from Clydebank, although I was born and brought up in Blairdardie, the posh bit of Drumchapel, Glasgow, if that's not a contradiction.

I have vivid memories of the walk from Singer station down Bannerman Street, and vivid memories of many of the games, not to mention the players: Jimmy Caskie, Alan Hunter, Dougie Hay, Sam Goodwin, Mike Larnach, Gregor Abel, Norrie Hall, and the irrepressible, and highly unlikely, Bobby Love.

I saw Andy Roxburgh rifle in an amazing goal from left

of the penalty box (Bankie's Club end); watched mesmerised from a range of about two feet, hanging over the advertising hoardings as Davie Cooper did his stuff; cowered as Clyde fans outside the ground lobbed half-bricks over the terrace roof in an un-guided missile kind of way.

Saw Alan Hunter stare at a hopeful hoof from our keeper (Mike McDonald) descending out of the floodlights before trapping it in one under his boot, swivelling and hammering it into the bottom corner; watched in utter amazement as Bobby Love, who had been mercilessly sherracked all game by the guy standing beside me, finally had enough and started sherracking him back in ragtime from the touchline (I think he got sent off for that).

Stood in the snow on Boxing Day 1968 (I think) with 21 other people (I counted them) as Brechin City not only beat us 2–1, which was bad enough, but had more heart, which was just not on. We would have gubbed them, if the players could've been arsed. They weren't. It still hurts, today.

Alan Cameron

Kilbowie Park

LAYER ROAD – COLCHESTER UNITED

Name:

Layer Road

Highest attendance:

19,072, vs. Reading,
27 November 1948

First league match:

Colchester United 0–0 Bristol Rovers,
26 August 1950

Final league match:

Colchester United 0–1 Stoke City,
26 April 2008

Memorable moment:

Colchester United 3–2 Leeds United,
13 February 1971 (FA Cup fifth round)

Current stadium:

The Colchester Community Stadium

Layer Road has been described as everything from 'modest' to 'ramshackle', but it was the battleground for Essex side Colchester United for seven decades. Originally inhabited by rivals Colchester Town, United benefited from their dissolution in 1937 when they moved in.

Just a year into their tenancy, the Layer Road End roof was blown off by a relentless wind, damaging some surrounding housing. But the repairs were swift, and the stand – a low covered terrace barely taller than the goal in front of it – was renovated using old wood from the demolished Popular Side Stand in the 1940s. A storm claimed the roof again a decade later, but this time a steel shortage prevented an immediate restoration. After initially shelving plans owing to cost, Layer Road was fitted with floodlights in 1959, thanks to proceeds from a lucrative FA Cup tie with Arsenal.

By the turn of the 1980s plans were drawn up to improve the ground's capacity and facilities, but these were rejected by the council, whose restrictions meant Colchester required a new stadium away from Layer Road. A reduction in capacity in the 1980s coincided with low attendance and compounded the situation, resulting in Colchester dropping out of the League in 1990.

Layer Road was reacquainted with League football after just two seasons, and the Clock End was covered and fitted with seats in 1996 after the club had sold the ground back to Colchester Council to ease debts in 1990, a consequence of relegation that season. As United soared to the Championship in 2006, a capacity of just over 6,000 highlighted the need for a new home, and planning permission was granted for a stadium to be built at Cuckoo Farm in March 2006.

Colchester's farewell to Layer Road was in sombre circumstances as they hosted Stoke City, knowing they were heading for League One and their brand new Colchester Community Stadium would be hosting third-tier football. Though now having to create new history for their new home, Colchester can no longer be accused of having a ground not befitting League football.

MEMORIES

I grew up in different parts of Germany and the UK as my father was in the forces. When my dad came home one day and said we were moving from Germany to England, I asked 'Where to this time'? 'Colchester!' he said. 'Where is that?' I thought. It was the summer of 1976 and I checked the table to see if Colchester had a football team. They did and they had just been relegated to Division Four. Very uninspiring!

Being 13 was a difficult age to make new friends but I was about to fall in love for the very first time. The new season kicked off and I remember walking from the army estate on a Tuesday night in August to Layer Road and watching the Us, as I would affectionately refer to them as for ever more, beat Halifax Town 3–0.

From that day on I was hooked. More than three decades later I have hardly missed a game. I loved Layer Road – the away teams and their fans hated it. I witnessed home games against Manchester United in 1979 and again in 1982. But you have to be careful what you wish for in life. Layer Road is no more and in its place on the other side of town overlooking the A12 is the Weston Homes Community Stadium: 10,000 seats, giant screen, executive boxes and the ability to generate funds to pay for record transfers.

I remember beating Grimsby under the Layer Road floodlights in 1980 to go top of the old Division Three and then after the match dashing to the University of Essex to catch The Boys' encore followed by the legendary Ramones at their peak. What a night! Saint and Greavsie featured the game next day on their lunchtime show. Happy days!

Steve Green

HIGHFIELD ROAD – COVENTRY CITY

Name:

Highfield Road

Highest attendance:

51, 455, vs. Wolverhampton Wanderers, 29 April 1967

First league match:

Coventry City 0–5 Tottenham Hotspur, 30 August 1919

Final league match:

Coventry City 6–2 Derby County, 30 April 2005

Memorable moment:

Coventry City 3–1 Millwall, 13 May 1967 (Coventry win Second Division title)

Current stadium:

The Ricoh Arena

Coventry City spent over 100 years at Highfield Road, straddling three centuries. They arrived in 1899 after brief spells at nearby Dowells Field and Stoke Road. The stadium was frequently a site of innovation in British football, and it holds the notable distinction of being England's first all-seater stadium despite reverting back to terracing four years later.

In 1935, 15 years after gaining entry to the League, a new Main Stand was constructed that would last just over 30 years before it was destroyed by fire. A new Main Stand was built within four months, complete with restaurant and striking aluminium roof, characteristic of Coventry's attention-grabbing activity on and off the pitch in the 1960s under manager Jimmy Hill.

This included large sections of the ground being rebuilt and redeveloped in a short space of time; four years prior to the new Main Stand, the North Stand was constructed to face it, followed by a two-tiered West Stand behind the goal on Coventry's promotion to the First Division in 1967. The 1980s saw the popular East Terrace brought in line to become all-seater, but the trial lasted four years as they were removed in 1985. Eight years later in 1993 a new stand was erected in its place, costing over £4 million.

Throughout the 1990s Highfield Road regularly hosted top-flight football as Coventry were founder members of the Premier League, but 2001 saw relegation. City moved to their purpose-built new home, the Ricoh Arena, with a seated capacity of 32,500, in 2005. Their last game was a 6–2 drubbing of Derby County. The site was used for housing development with the area of the pitch being retained and re-turfed for the residents.

MEMORIES

It's the morning of 30th April 2005. I was making the long journey up to Coventry from my home in Farnham. Today is the day that Highfield Road hosts its last ever competitive football match – Coventry City vs. Derby County. I'd followed Coventry City from a small boy, falling in love with the club my father supported.

As we approached Coventry on the A46 we all became very aware of our fellow Sky Blue fans travelling to the game. Many of the homes near to the ground had City flags flying. Outside it was unusually empty – everybody wanted to soak up the Highfield Road atmosphere one last time.

We entered the ground at the corner of the North and West Stands through the turnstiles set forward from the stands rather than into them. Usually at around 2.15pm on a match day the stands are normally empty as fans enjoy a few beers and pies away, but not today.

On normal match days the noise within the ground was pretty loud, but today there was a great buzz that was infectious. If I were a Derby fan that day, I would have been a little overawed – it was only a few seasons before that they themselves had moved to their new home at Pride Park.

As the game kicked off, the buzz in the ground didn't die down – it got louder! In the 20th minute Gary McSheffrey made a great run into the box and finished with a low shot into the bottom left corner. He followed this nine minutes later with a penalty after a clumsy challenge by ex-Coventry player Mo Konjic. By half-time Dele Adebola and Stern John had put the Sky Blues four up!

The second half saw Derby's Bolder unleash an unstoppable shot from all of 25 yards. But Coventry wasted no time restoring their lead through Stern John, and while Derby's Peschisolido scored again Coventry rightfully had the last word through Andrew Whing – 6–2! The fans in the South Stand went wild as Whing ran along the front of the stand doing his best airplane impression!

When the final whistle blew, though, fans were on the pitch instantly, celebrating with the players, dancing and grabbing any memorabilia they could. There could have been no better end to a football ground than this; in front of its final full house, Highfield Road got to witness eight very good goals, beautiful sunshine and very passionate supporters who, for the last 106 years, called this stadium home.

Leaving the party at last, I wondered would the new stadium – the Ricoh Arena – be able to hold such fond memories? It's a little sad to drive up to the ground past where Highfield Road once stood; it has now been turned into a housing estate. It also unfortunately suffered a fire during its dismantling.

Having now visited the Ricoh Arena a few times, it is now becoming home. But in 106 years' time what memories will it hold?

Dennis Cartwright

FEETHAMS – DARLINGTON

Name:

Feethams

Highest attendance:

21,023, vs. Bolton Wanderers,

14 November 1960

First league match:

Darlington 2–0 Halifax Town,

27 August 1921

Final league match:

Darlington 2–2 Leyton Orient,

3 May 2003

Memorable moment:

Darlington 4–1 Chelsea,

29 January 1958

(FA Cup fourth round replay)

Current stadium:

The Darlington Arena

Darlington spent 120 years at Feethams, alongside the town's cricket club. The two grounds stood side by side, with fans having to walk through Darlington's 'twin towers' and around the cricket field to get to the football action. The stadium was a throwback to football's early days, fitting for a team that had been residents of England's fourth tier for two decades.

The East Stand was the most impressive, built in 1997 with 'Darlington' adorning the black and white seats. Its predecessor had been erected in 1919, taking five years to build owing to the club's financial situation, and only ran along two-thirds of the pitch. But the construction of the new East Stand almost crippled Darlington financially.

The West Stand had a more eventful history. Originally built at the turn of the 20th century, it was destroyed by fire on the night of Darlington's first floodlit match, a 5–2 triumph over Millwall in 1960. An electrical fault was blamed, and an exact replica was constructed the following year, keeping the sense of history of the ground. The North Stand, or 'Tin Shed' as it was known, accommodated the more vocal home fans and backed onto the cricket ground; the Polam Lane End terrace opposite was open to the elements.

Chairman George Reynolds eventually moved the Quakers to the 25,500 all-seater Darlington Arena in 2003, though he left the club under a cloud shortly after it opened and administration followed. The new stadium has a record attendance of 11,600, set during a Division 3 game against Kidderminster Harriers in 2003, and an average of around 4,000. The inevitable occurred in 2010 as Darlington were docked points after going into administration and dropped out of the Football League.

MEMORIES

My particular memory was the send-off that Feethams got; my friend 'GeordieQuaker' and a few others organised the Tin Shed on tour for the last four home games of the season. It was a simple concept: all the singers from the Tin Shed/North Terrace would move around the ground for each game. Special T-shirts were printed with 'Farewell Feethams' and 'Thanks for the Memories'.

Starting in the newest stand, The East Stand – all-seated – for a game with Bury, then the South Terrace for Shrewsbury Town and the West Stand – typically away fans only – for the visit of Hull, which led to a conga line around the stand when we went 1–0 up!

Led on by GQ and his drum, we partied – fuelled by significant amounts of ale – around the ground with each game, and the last game at Feethams saw us back in the crumbling Tin Shed for the visit of Leyton Orient. Many wore fancy dress, and the atmosphere was outstanding. The inevitable pitch invasion at the end led to a huge football match on the turf, and the occasional watering eye!

The flag that was left on a floodlight as everyone left summed the craziness up -

'The Tin Shed on tour'. We stayed until the end'.

ShrewsX

I've some great memories of the old girl. My first memory was of what I think was my first match – the 1982 'save the Quakers' charity game vs. Southampton (I was six years old) when Lawrie McMenemy's Saints came up to play us. Keegan was the star in their team and we had David Speedie playing for us at the time. Speedie got a hat-trick in a 5–3 win. I can't remember much more about it other than when the players came out they kicked footballs into the crowd and threw sweets to the kids as well. I thought every game was going to be like that at the time!

Another fond memory was the changing of ends at half time. Before Hillsborough, etc, you were able to choose the end which Darlo were shooting to and then at half-time walk around the back of the main stand and go to the other end of the ground for the second half. I think we were the last Football League club who allowed this to happen and I was gutted when this was no longer allowed. Even though I was only in my early teens I still recognised it as a sign of the way the game was going.

Obviously the couple of promotions I've experienced were the greatest memories I have. I just wish we'd have stayed there since the new ground, whilst being a perfect example of how crazy the game has become, is literally killing us as a club, for numerous reasons which I won't go into.

Richard Tearle

BASEBALL GROUND – DERBY COUNTY

Name:
Baseball Ground
Highest attendance:
41,826, vs. Tottenham Hotspur,
20 September 1969
First league match:
Derby County 0–1 Sunderland,
19 March 1892
Final league match:
Derby County 1–3 Arsenal,
11 May 1997
Memorable moment:
Derby County 1–0 Liverpool,
1 May 1972
(Derby win the First Division title)
Current stadium:
Pride Park

Former League Champions and FA Cup winners Derby County called the Baseball Ground home for over a century. As its name suggests, the stadium was used to play a sport more commonly associated with America. Derby's first League match at the ground was in 1892 – a 1–0 defeat to Sunderland – after there was a fixture clash at the Racecourse Ground. They moved in permanently in 1895, sharing with Derby County Baseball Club, but it wouldn't be for long as their bat-and-ball-playing co-habitants folded three years later.

The man who owned the stadium and tried to interest the population of Derby in baseball, Sir Francis Ley, sold the Baseball Ground to County in 1924, after which the club went about erecting four covered stands in the space of a decade. The construction of a main stand was followed by two stands behind the goals, the Osmaston and Normanton Ends, which were almost mirror images of each other, except that the latter slanted backwards from the pitch, a quirk from the days of baseball.

During the construction of the three stands, plans for a new multi-purpose stadium were already being proposed, but bomb damage to the Osmaston End during World War II but paid to this. A new East Stand was built in 1969 named in honour of Ley, and three years later the stadium witnessed Derby win the League twice in quick succession in 1972 and 1975 – the club's finest hour.

The hemmed-in stadium had a reduced capacity of 18,000 following the Taylor Report, and in consequence County, then in the Premier League, moved to the 33,000-capacity Pride Park Stadium on the outskirts of town in 1997. The Baseball Ground would remain in use for County reserve games before it was demolished in 2003, where housing was planned in its place. The new purpose-built home would be for football only, where fans would be hoping it would be goals, not home runs, raining in.

MEMORIES

I went to my first Derby game on 18th October 1973 – we drew 0–0 with Leeds. We did not have a car so my Dad, brother and myself went the 20 or so miles from South Normanton on two buses. And as a seven-year-old what felt like a long trek from Derby bus station.

We arrived close to kick-off time and queued up outside the Ossie End for the terraces. When we finally got to the front of the queue the chap on the turnstiles turned us away saying the ground was full. My Dad pleaded with him to let us in, explaining the time it had taken to get there. Eventually the chap relented and let us in but warned my Dad that the kids wouldn't be able to see as we would be stood at the back.

He was right, but some people in the Ossie middle tier noticed us and got the fans below to lift my brother and me up so we could stand in front of their seats and watch the game. We had a good view although I can't really remember the game. The following Sunday when we looked in the newspaper the official attendance was 36,003. It might have been a coincidence but we always claimed we were the three. Don't think anything like this would happen today.

Pinxtonram

BELLE VUE – DONCASTER ROVERS

Name:
Belle Vue

Highest attendance:
37,149, vs. Hull City,
2 October 1948

First league match:
Doncaster 0–0 Wigan Borough,
25 August 1923

Final league match:
Doncaster 1–0 Nottingham Forest,
23 December 2006

Memorable moment:
Doncaster 10–0 Darlington,
25 January 1964 (record League victory)

Current stadium:
Keepmoat Stadium

Doncaster Rovers moved into Belle Vue from their Bennetthorpe Ground in 1922. The ground had an eventful history, and witnessed Doncaster rocket up the League at the turn of the century, though Rovers moved out before their ascent to the Coca-Cola Championship. The stadium went out with a bang in 2007, a year after its tenants had left, when gas filled the ground after a boiler was stolen; the resulting explosion sped up the demolition process.

A trace of Rovers' Bennetthorpe history could still be seen at Belle Vue as late as 1985; upon arriving in 1922 the club transported the Main Stand from their old home on wheels and deposited it on the North Terrace behind the goal. It was demolished after the fire at Valley Parade, when wooden stands were finally deemed unsafe, despite countless other incidents across the country prior to the Bradford tragedy.

Despite this precaution Belle Vue's Main Stand was set ablaze a decade later, with then-chairman Ken Richardson later arrested and charged with arson; a court later found he hired a former SAS soldier to douse it in petrol. The extensive fire damage was said to have been a factor in Doncaster dropping out of the Football League in 1999.

However, after a period languishing in the football abyss, Rovers rose like a phoenix from the flames as they secured back-to-back promotions and found themselves in League One by 2004. Their move to the Keepmoat Stadium in 2006 didn't stall their momentum as they secured another promotion in 2008 to the Championship, just five years after returning to the Football League.

A year later came another flame-related incident when, as previously mentioned, the Main Stand, which had survived the arson attempt a dozen years earlier, exploded after the aforementioned boiler theft. Though Belle Vue had long since been abandoned, it was the exclamation mark on a residency for a club whose story wouldn't be out of place in a soap opera.

MEMORIES

Belle Vue was a hole...but I loved her. My memory of her is walking up the muddy pot-holed path on a night game and getting the smell of football up my nostrils. It's a weird smell, a combination of burgers, fags, cigars and Bovril, but nice all the same and it added to the excitement of what only football can bring.

Belle Vue could be a volatile place sometimes – even Neil Warnock once said that he loved the place for its atmosphere and banter with the home fans. I remember Danny Sonner of Port Vale at the time having a torrid afternoon; the fans in the Pop Side started chanting his name in a very low, monotone and repetitive way. It sounded like a thousand insane monks waiting to be fed the heart of a pagan virgin. Anyway, once he caught the low rumbling of his name in his ears he stopped in his tracks and looked across at us in the Popular Side with his head tilted slightly to the left and a blank, quizzical look on his face. It completely put him off his game and was duly subbed in the second half.

I've seen some dross in my time at Belle Vue but one of my favourite memories is of the Snodin brothers holding the Conference League Cup above their heads in the Main Stand with every fan either in the stand or in front of it celebrating together. I think it was more of a celebration of the fact that we still had a football club; it was a very emotional night.

I wish the old girl could have entertained Championship football, with a bit of a face-lift of course. I miss seeing all the regulars who had their own spot on the terracing (mine was half way along Pop Side, four steps from top), I miss the surge of the crowd when we scored or hit the bar with a 25-yard screamer, I miss being stood with like-minded people who scream and shout obscenities at the opposition and have no voice left after a game.

When we moved house, it felt like the club had lost a bit of its soul. Old Belle Vue, I miss you.
Nudga

BOGHEAD PARK – DUMBARTON

Name:

Boghead Park

Highest attendance:

18,001, vs. Raith Rovers,
2 March 1957

First league match:

Dumbarton 1–1 Cowlairs,
16 August 1890

Final league match:

Dumbarton 2–1 East Fife,
6 May 2000

Memorable moment:

Dumbarton 4–2 Berwick Rangers,
3 May 1972 (Dumbarton win Second Division title)

Current stadium:

Strathclyde Homes Stadium

Boghead Park was the subject of neglect in its later years, but the quirky, ramshackle ground was one of the oldest in existence when in use; Dumbarton arrived in 1879 before leaving for their new home in 2000. Like the team, Boghead's finest moments came early on in its existence, with the club describing their 'halcyon' days as the first decade of the 20th century.

At its peak Boghead could accommodate 20,000 spectators, though it was rarely filled; owing to Premier Division regulations the capacity was limited to just half that for Dumbarton's one-season sojourn in the Scottish top flight, and upon relegation in 1985 the capacity was gradually constricted as they dropped down the League.

A slice of Hollywood came to the not-so-glamorous Boghead in 2000 as the ground was used as the home of fictional team Kilnockie FC in A Shot At Glory starring former Rangers hero Ally McCoist, as the film showed them trying to reach the Scottish Cup final while struggling to stay in existence. The run-down stadium fitted in with the team's lowly status in the film, if not quite a cause for pride amongst the Dumbarton faithful.

Plans to sell Boghead also had an effect on the upkeep of the stadium. Little maintenance was performed in its later years, as illustrated by greenery creeping up from the terraces. Brief plans to create a new stadium on the site were briskly scrapped and in 2000 Dumbarton moved to the vastly more picturesque Strathclyde Homes Stadium. Situated next to Dumbarton Castle, itself nestled in the middle of the 240-foot-high Dumbarton rock, that overlooks the Sons' new home, the one-sided stadium would require much less attention; though it was unlikely the 2,000-capacity crowd would notice anyway.

MEMORIES

A sense of the old glory days returned yesterday to Boghead Park, home of Dumbarton FC, as hundreds of fans queued to act as extras in Hollywood legend Robert Duvall's movie tribute to Scottish football.

In recent years fans of the Third Division team have had little to shout about, with the club making the headlines more often because of the regularity of cancellations because of a waterlogged pitch at Boghead.

Attendances now average about 600 and local residents say they are hardly aware of when the team is playing at home.

Yesterday, however, the ground was busy again, with fans keen to be involved in a film that tells the story of a fictional small town team's bid for Scottish Cup glory.

Duvall, famed for his Godfather role, turned out, as well as Scottish football great Ally McCoist who stars in the film.

Others in the cast include Alec Baldwin, Billy Connolly, and Manchester United manager Sir Alex Ferguson, who has a cameo role in the film.

For once the weather was kind and there was no threat of the ground being ruled unplayable, as around 1,400 Sons fans of all ages, bedecked in black and gold colours, some with faces painted, waited outside the ground in anticipation of the 3pm kick-off.

The Glasgow Herald, July 1999

BAYVIEW PARK – EAST FIFE

Name:
Bayview

Highest attendance:
22,515, vs. Raith Rovers,
2 January 1950

First league match:
East Fife 1–2 Bathgate,
20 August 1921

Final league match:
East Fife 0–1 Forfar Athletic,
9 May 1998

Memorable moment:
East Fife 4–1 Glasgow Celtic,
21 March 1953 (famous League win)

Current stadium:
Bayview Stadium

Bayview housed the Scottish Football League's longest-serving members from 1903 to 1998. Originally named Town Hall Park, East Fife took over in 1903 from then-incumbents Leven Thistle and renamed the ground – having been usurped, Thistle promptly folded. Shortly afterwards the ground became fully enclosed with a stand, but several failed League applications followed.

Housing developments and the construction of a school threatened to usurp the usurpers in the years to follow, so in 1910 Bayview was moved to the west to accommodate the school with the stand on the north terrace now at the northeast of the ground. A big money cup-tie against Celtic the following year saw improvements to the banking and a new capacity of 11,000.

East Fife were finally successful in their pursuit of League Football in 1921, and set about improving the pitch. Plans for a new stand and extended terracing were realised a year later, the new stand facing, rather than replacing, Bayview's original. As East Fife progressed up the League pyramid, Bayview was also improved, with extended terracing around the north and east sides of the ground.

The club's best days were immediately after World War II, with four League Cup final appearances, of which three were won. East Fife would finish third in the Scottish First Division in 1953, missing out on the League title by four points to Rangers, but would never reach those giddy heights again, nor would Bayview be filled to the tune of 22,000 again. East Fife left for the new Bayview Stadium in 1998, another one-sided affair with the opportunity to expand if they ever soar to the heights of the 1940s and '50s again.

MEMORIES

I am 59 and remember when I was probably about 12 I heard about a pre-season private friendly at old Bayview against Dundee – then the best side in Scotland.

They had just won the League. I sneaked in sometime before the match and Alan Gilzean – soon to be of Spurs – was on the pitch in his civvies. To cut a long story short, he invited me onto the pitch and took a penalty against me. In my mind, I made a brilliant save but I know at least I saved it against the best centre-forward in Scotland – soon arguably to be the best centre-forward in England. Ian Ure – soon to move to England too – really made his life a misery as they walked off the pitch!
Bruce Mitchell

BROCKVILLE PARK – FALKIRK

Name:
Brockville Park

Highest attendance:
23,100, vs. Glasgow Celtic,
21 February 1953

First league match:
Falkirk 0–1 St Bernard's,
23 August 1902

Final league match:
Falkirk 2–3 Inverness Caledonian Thistle,
10 May 2003

Memorable moment:
Falkirk 2–1 Clyde, 2 March 1957
(Scottish Cup quarter-final)

Current stadium:
Falkirk Stadium

Brockville Park was home to Falkirk from 1885 and was held in high regard by the club's fans; it was considered an intimidating place for visiting teams. But the ground hindered the club's progression in its later years; by not reaching SPL requirements, Falkirk were denied promotion twice – in 2001 and 2003 – despite winning the League on the latter occasion.

The ground was characterised by the Cooperage Lane and Watson Street terracing behind the goals. They started at a point and expanded as they wrapped around the pitch, giving the ground the look of a trophy from the air. The Main Stand ran down the west side of the pitch, whilst opposite was known as The Shed.

The decision to leave was a necessary one, and in 2003 Falkirk vacated Brockville, taking the First Division title with them but again no promotion. A Morrisons supermarket was erected in place of the ground, with several features being incorporated and retained, including an old turnstile.

After a season sharing the Ochilview Stadium with Stenhousemuir they moved in to their purpose-built Falkirk Stadium. The move paid off as Falkirk won the title in their first season at their new ground, finally gaining promotion to the Scottish Premier League.

MEMORIES

I've been a Falkirk supporter since the age of seven and I first attended the old Brockville Park in 1970. My first game was a pre-season friendly that saw Falkirk play Everton. Those were the days; big crowds in a small stuffy stadium. Heaven knows what Everton thought of it. The picture here is from 1905 and what is most remarkable is how little the place changed in the 65 years between then and my first visit. When a youngster I always took my place just below the window of the house you can see in the image. Later I graduated to the 'choir' in the shed and then up onto the mighty bank of the Hope Street End. Happy days.

Gordon Cameron

REDHEUGH PARK – GATESHEAD

Name:
Redheugh Park

Highest attendance:
20,752, vs. Lincoln City,
25 September 1937

First league match:
Gateshead 2–1 Doncaster Rovers,
30 August 1930

Final league match:
Gateshead 3–0 Walsall,
25 April 1960

Memorable moment:
Gateshead 1–0 Liverpool,
10 January 1953
(FA Cup third round)

Current stadium:
Gateshead International Stadium (Gateshead FC)

In a part of the country where the supporters are famed for their passion for the game, there was once another venue for fans in the North East to view League football – Redheugh Park, home of Gateshead AFC.

Born from the ashes of South Shields FC, who relocated in search of greater support, Gateshead kicked off in the Third Division at Redheugh in 1930. The oval-shaped stadium with terracing throughout was built specifically for their arrival. Cover was provided on each side except the Ropery Road End terrace.

Gateshead were another club to allow greyhound racing to occupy their home as a means of boosting revenue and allow for maintenance of the stadium, though the inclusion of the track and totaliser behind the Ropery Road End saw the pitch and terrace size reduced.

With crowds steadily dwindling and success on the pitch not forthcoming, Gateshead finished 22nd in the Fourth Division in 1960 and were forced to apply for re-election along with Southport, Hartlepool and Oldham. Despite their confidence they were not successful and dropped out of League competition.

Eleven years later the stadium's state of disrepair coupled with a fire saw Gateshead relocate to the International Athletics Stadium, though their tenure there was to be short-lived; the club went into liquidation in 1973. Redheugh Park had been demolished a year previously, with football returning in 1991 in the form of a six-a-side centre.

A reformed South Shields FC, then playing in the Northern Premier League, relocated to the International Athletics Stadium in 1974 and became Gateshead United FC, although this was short-lived and the club went out of business just three years later. A new Gateshead FC was formed to take their place, and it is this incarnation that has endured to this day.

MEMORIES

A fifth round victory away to Plymouth Argyle] set up the biggest game in Gateshead's history – the FA Cup quarter-final at home to Bolton Wanderers. Cup fever hit the Town like never before with thousands queuing as tickets went on sale at Gateshead Town Hall.

One woman had to have her leg amputated because of injuries sustained in the stampede for tickets. 17,692 fans turned up for the game as Gateshead changed from their regular all-white shirts to an unfamiliar Newcastle United-style black'n'white striped top.

The team played their hearts out and could possibly have won the game late on when Bolton defender Bell handled inside the penalty box (he later admitted the offence), but the referee waved play-on. Bolton broke away and England International Nat Lofthouse headed in past Bob Gray to break the home fans' hearts.

Homeoftheheed.co.uk

RAYDALE PARK – GRETNA

Name:

Raydale Park

Highest attendance:

3,000, vs. Dundee United,
17 January 2005

First league match:

Gretna 1–1 Greenock Morton,
3 August 2002

Final league match:

Gretna 0–0 Clyde,
21 April 2007

Memorable moment:

Gretna 1–0 St Mirren,
25 February 2006 (Scottish Cup quarter-final)

Current stadium:

N/A

Raydale Park was the scene of the modern football fairytale that was Gretna FC. Traditionally known as a romantic wedding venue for eloping couples, Gretna wrote its name into football folklore when its football team rose to the summit of the Scottish game in 2007. Though Raydale never hosted a Scottish Premier League fixture, failing to meet SPL requirements, it mattered not as within a year the club was liquidated and dropped out of the League completely.

Gretna had played at Raydale Park since their formation in 1946, playing under the jurisdiction of the English FA owing to its proximity to the Anglo-Scottish border. In 2002, such is the rich tapestry of football, they crossed paths with Airdrieonians as they replaced them in the Scottish Football League. Raydale then witnessed an unprecedented three successive promotions from 2005 to 2007, sending fans into dreamland.

The ground itself was largely standing, with cover on the Main Stand, and its counterpart running the length of the other side of the pitch, and the imaginatively titled Long Stand behind the goal. The away terrace opposite was open to the elements. It was for this reason Raydale never saw Gretna's swansong in the top flight, the facilities having barely improved from the club's non-League days despite the millions pumped in by benefactor Brooks Mileson. It was Mileson's ill health and eventual death that also sounded the death knell for Gretna.

Gretna shared Motherwell's Fir Park for their sole season amongst the elite, despite the round-trip for fans being over 100 miles. Raydale Park was sold by administrators after the club's demise in 2008, and the new owners have allowed their successors – supporter-owned Gretna 2008 FC – to play there temporarily, the ground and club having come full circle in just a few short years.

MEMORIES

The millionaire who funded Gretna's rise from obscurity died yesterday at the age of 60 after battling with a series of illnesses. Brooks Mileson lived just five more months after the club with which he was synonymous lost their own fight for survival in June last year. And, sadly, there is no one left to mourn him.

There will no minute's silence at Raydale Park, or players gathered around the centre circle in tribute. The man who could easily have been tagged The Pied Piper of Gretna, who lured 12,000 people to Hampden Park to support his 'village team' in the 2006 Scottish Cup final against Heart of Midlothian, will receive none of the usual trappings accorded to those who worked in the game.

True, Raydale Park will be cloaked in silence. It has been silent every day since Gretna FC was liquidated by the administrators with debts of £4 million after a torrid one-season tenure in the Clydesdale Bank Premier League. The players and the staff disappeared after being made redundant and Gretna gave up the Scottish Football League membership that defined a town of fewer than 3,000 souls.

Phil Gordon, *The Times* (November 2008)

Gretna's incredible rise to fame continued yesterday when they reached the semi-finals of the Scottish Cup – the first Second Division club since 1982 to reach the last four.

A Kenny Deuchar goal in the 73rd minute sparked wild celebrations at Raydale Park as the Borders side ousted First Division leaders St Mirren from the tournament.

It was quite an achievement for an outfit that only joined the Scottish League in 2002, won the Third Division in their third term and currently lead the Second.

***Sunday Times*, February 2006**

THE SHAY – HALIFAX TOWN

Name:
The Shay

Highest attendance:
36,885, vs. Tottenham Hotspur,
14 February 1953

First league match:
Halifax Town 5–1 Darlington,
3 September 1921

Final league match:
Halifax Town 2–4 Rushden & Diamonds FC,
20 April 2002

Memorable moment:
Halifax Town 1-0 Stoke City
31 January 1953 (FA Cup fourth round)

Current stadium:
N/A

The Shay spent most of its Football League existence in a rather dilapidated state; work on renovating the stadium was never top of the list for a club whose primary objective was to retain League status. It was during its second stint as a League venue that work began to pick up and continued even after its tenant, Halifax Town AFC, went out of business in 2008.

The stadium was completed in time for Halifax's debut season in the League, 1921–22, and had a stunning opening match, the hosts beating Darlington 5–0. Its Main Stand was purchased from Manchester City, still at their old stadium of Hyde Road, while behind the goal was open terracing.

In the late 1940s the Shay introduced speedway to its repertoire, yet the track proved bothersome for football as even the fans at the front of the stands were still 30 feet away from the pitch, hindering the stadium's acoustics. It is said one Halifax manager wanted to play crowd noise from Wembley over the tannoy to improve the atmosphere!

The stadium was a hindrance for the club; several former chairmen attempted to sell it to supermarkets and property developers but it was the fans and the arrival of Halifax's Rugby League club that allowed the ground to finally be brought up to date. Upon Halifax's return to the League after a six-year absence in 1998 a new South Stand complete with cantilever roof was built behind the goal, and work on a new Main Stand on the east side had begun.

Unfortunately for the club and stadium, work stalled on the East Stand and it remained unfinished and was due for completion at the end of 2009, a lengthy wait. Halifax Town AFC were wound up in 2008 after mounting debts proved insurmountable. FC Halifax Town replaced them and went on to play at the ground in the Northern Premier League Division One (North) in 2008–09.

The Shay looks the best it has for years and, with a football club with fresh impetus for success, it is not impossible that the revamped ground could host League football once again.

MEMORIES

For three-quarters of a century, Halifax Town stood as a monument to failure, a decaying stadium with a team to match. And then it happened. As others turned a blind, uncaring eye, the fans packed the terraces of the Shay to give the last rites to their club; oblivion beckoned and an oblivious world prepared to relegate them to the asterisks of football history (Halifax Town FC lost League status 1993, subsequently vanished).

There were 7,451 present on that sad, sunlit spring afternoon, when a player they had once employed scored the goal that gave Hereford United a 1–0 win and finally relieved Halifax of their membership of the Football League, kicking them off the ledge that they had clung to for so many desperate seasons, when mediocrity and near-bankruptcy went hand in hand.

Twelve times they had had to apply for re-election, so at least they would save the cost of a stamp, but fans still lingered and wept long into the night.

Neither has the intervening five years been much kinder. All bar around 800 of those supporters had since decided that there are better ways of spending a Saturday afternoon than watching their team being thrashed. Indeed, on the final day of last season, only a dramatic victory over Stevenage Borough prevented Halifax from having to rub shoulders with the mighty men of the Unibond League.

But, ten months on, the club they thought had died is in rare good health. Where once they had to lock fans in to get a decent crowd, on Saturday they had to lock them out, 3,951 people cramming into every available orifice at the Shay for the visit of Rushden and Diamonds, with a couple of hundred more perched on the various free vantage points that the hills above the ground provide. And this time the tears were of joy.
The Times, March 1998

DOUGLAS PARK – HAMILTON ACADEMICAL

Name:

Douglas Park

Highest attendance:

28,690, vs. Heart of Midlothian,

3 March 1937

First league match:

Hamilton Academical 2–3 Kilmarnock,

6 November 1897

Final league match:

Hamilton Academical 2–1 Dumbarton,

14 May 1994

Memorable moment:

Hamilton Academical 1–1 Meadowbank Thistle,

7 May 1988

(Hamilton promoted to Scottish Premier League)

Current stadium:

New Douglas Park

A team with one of the more interesting names in football resided at the more sternly titled Douglas Park for 106 years of their existence, arriving in 1888. The characteristic ground with its uncovered goal-end terraces was never considered a problem until two brief seasons in the Premier Division exactly a century after moving in convinced the club that their home would not be sufficient for further top-flight exploits.

As with a lot of clubs in the 1990s, Hamilton's departure from Douglas Park was ultimately due to the Taylor Report, and the ground not meeting the requirements of the Scottish Premier League. The Accies' aspirations for top-flight football caused them to leave for a new stadium, and Britain got another supermarket in its place.

The new stadium didn't materialise straight away and the Accies found themselves ground-sharing for a seven-year period before moving into the L-shaped New Douglas Park, located just behind the old one, in 2001. The Accies, like Falkirk and Dumbarton, left their four-sided home for a modern and cautious alternative with only two sides – only time will tell if it was a smart decision.

MEMORIES

Anyone remember a crucial end-of-season match against Clyde (pretty sure it was 1982–83 season when the recently departed Brian McLaughlin scored eight goals to keep us up)? In this game we won 4–1 but it was a real nerve shredder to begin with as we missed at least one penalty, possibly two. We wore sky blue as we usually did at home to Clyde and Pat Nevin played for them. Can't remember any of the goals but I've a feeling Jamie Fairlie scored a belter.
Beardedgoalie

My earliest memory of the Shed was a midweek game against Airdrie in the 1970s. There was no fence and the fans were separated by no more than a few feet and three fairly nervous cops! The fashion in those days was to tie your scarves round your wrists and I also remember wondering why some guys were wearing builders' hardhats decorated in Accies colours. The answer soon became clear as bricks were lobbed from each side of the police cordon; happy days.
Shammy

My first ever game was against Raith as a nine-year-old but the ones that stick in my mind are the 3–2 against Airdrie when we were down to eight men, the 9–1 against Brechin and the Reserve Cup final against Rangers.
Rexclark

LEEDS ROAD – HUDDERSFIELD TOWN

Name:
Leeds Road

Highest attendance:
67,037, vs. Arsenal,
27 February 1932

First league match:
Huddersfield Town 0–1 Burnley,
10 September 1910

Final league match:
Huddersfield Town 2–1 Blackpool,
30 April 1994

Memorable moment:
Huddersfield Town 3–0 Millwall,
4 March 1922
(FA Cup quarter-final)

Current stadium:
Galpharm Stadium

Leeds Road was once home to the most feared team in England. When Huddersfield Town won their third League championship in a row less than 20 years after forming, their home ground was today's equivalent to Old Trafford. Acquired in 1908, it was little more than a field with an old tramcar doubling up as a changing room and a ticket office, but upon gaining entry to the Football League in 1910 Huddersfield began work on Leitch-inspired designs for a new stadium.

With the pitch rotated 90 degrees and a newly covered West Stand opened fully in 1911, Leeds Road had a capacity of 40,000, though this was seldom filled owing to the town's preference for Rugby League. Rapid spending coupled with disappointing gate returns saw Huddersfield slip into administration the following year, their future at Leeds Road seemingly in doubt.

The crisis was averted, however, and success on the pitch brought frequent attendance records. By the 1920s Leeds Road was the home of the English Champions with crowds regularly topping 30,000.

1950 saw the Main Stand ablaze after the northwest corner of the ground caught fire. Unlike nearby Bradford's tragic fire, however, the ground was empty save for a few hastily evacuated employees. Five years later a roof was erected on the mammoth East Terrace, covering 20,000 fans, and floodlights were installed in 1961. The creation of seating in the West Stand 'paddock' in 1970 gave Leeds Road the appearance it would keep until it was vacated 24 years later.

European football came to the ground in 1971 in the form of the Anglo-Italian Cup, but the club yo-yoed between the lower leagues for the next two decades, peppering the stadium with a variety of promotion highs and relegation lows. In 1994 Huddersfield left Leeds Road for the modern all-seater Galpharm Stadium (then known as the Alfred McAlpine Stadium). A retail park now stands on the site of Leeds Road, with a plaque marking the location of the old centre circle.

MEMORIES

The scoreboard behind the away end that only Carol Vorderman could work out, to the toilets in the terrace that meant pissing on the outside of someone's garden wall? And who could forget the highland toffee at the snack bar!

Officer Dibble

Coming down the hill at the back of the away-end looking for my first glimpse of the floodlights and the silhouettes of the away fans. Trying to guess how many they'd bring. Walking past the back of the Bradley Mills End and mingling with them. That long winding walkway of the east terrace complete with its own trees and streetlights, felt like climbing a mountain as a kid. I loved the place, always will.

Fitzyblue

Those horrible bags of 'fish'n'chips' you bought by the touchline.

My dad being a cop and insisting I got lifted over the turnstiles rather than paying.

The smell of Woodbine smoke wafting across the crowded masses.

Singing at Norman the St John's ambulance bloke who got weekly abuse from the Cowshed.

Pitch invasions after the last match of the season.

The climb up the steps before looking down the east terrace onto the pitch; the degradation only made it feel more homely.

Sitting on a blue barrier leaning against my Dad for the whole match, flanked by both my Granddads (RIP) who did the same all their lives.

'You Got It' by Roy Orbison, 'Something's Got A Hold Of My Heart' by Pitney and Almond before every match.

Genuine optimism that any team could win the First Division within about five years.

All the faces you came to recognise, whilst never knowing, over years of shared despair.

We never won anything, but great years. Thanks for the memories everyone.

Mr. X

BOOTHFERRY PARK – HULL CITY

Name:

Boothferry Park

Highest attendance:

55,019, vs. Manchester United,
26 February 1949

First league match:

Hull City 0–0 Lincoln City,
31 August 1946

Final league match:

Hull City 0–1 Darlington,
14 December 2002

Memorable moment:

Hull City 7–0 Barnsley,
7 October 1964
(first game with floodlights)

Current stadium:

KC Stadium

Hull City finally moved into Boothferry Park in 1946, nearly two decades after plans were initially drawn up in 1929. Several factors including financial difficulties and the outbreak of World War II hampered the move but, upon settling, City made up for lost time; Boothferry's 20,000 capacity when opened had been more than doubled to 55,000 when it witnessed its record crowd against Manchester United three years later.

The Main Stand and a partial cover on the North Stand behind the goal were in place for the ground's opening; the goal-side cover was completed in 1950. The following year the East Stand was erected, giving Boothferry 75 per cent cover. That same year saw the ground's very own railway station situated behind that East Stand open for business; Boothferry Halt was used for the first time for the visit of Everton. The mid-1960s saw a South Stand constructed with a gymnasium, making Boothferry Park the envy of most First Division clubs despite Hull City competing in the lower echelons of the League.

But this would prove to be the peak of the stadium's history; Hull would not make it to the First Division as many had expected, and gradually the capacity was reduced owing to Taylor Report implications. In 1982 the North Stand was replaced with a supermarket, echoing Bolton's Burnden Park.

The affectionate nicknames of 'Fer Ark', and 'Bothferry' – owing to various damaged signage around the stadium – was indicative of its best days being in the past. Hull moved out in 2002, taking up residence at the new KC Stadium, to be shared with Rugby League side Hull FC. It would be there that City would reach England's top tier, suggesting that City's new home's best days are indeed still ahead of it.

MEMORIES

When I was 14 or 15 years old, and working as a Saturday boy for the local butcher, the then admin manager invited me to experience my first live football match (my own Father was more of a snooker or F1 fan), Hull City vs. Doncaster Rovers.

I worked until 1pm, and then took the short train ride with him and a few others from Driffield (21 miles away) to Hull Paragon. I distinctly remember buying two tickets for the journey, 1 for the main leg, and a 2nd (50p return) from Paragon to Boothferry Halt. This short journey was as much a part of the experience as the game itself for me, as this was where the 'lads' came rolling out of the pub with 20 minutes before kick-off, armed with well lubricated voice box.

The singing started in earnest as the train pulled out of the station on its short journey to the ground. Upon arrival, what greeted me was the most amazing sensation I had, until that

time, experienced in my life. Off the train, searched, into the turnstile (£5.50 entry if I recall correctly), grab a programme and a pie and get ready for the team coming out – all within 50 yards of the exit from the train, and all timed to coincide within 10 minutes of kick-off.

Then the first experience of the Boothferry Roar – several thousand passionate supporters, packed inside a magnificent – although ageing – stadium, the like of which I had only seen on TV when watching Match of the Day or European/World Cup games with my Grandfather. I can't begin to describe the feeling of excitement and anticipation that I felt at that moment; the taste of pie in my mouth, my sweaty palms wrapped around my programme and the sheer thrill of being a part of this single mind – singing together, cheering together, almost breathing in union as a single entity.

We won that day – one of few victories that season – but the memory of that first visit was enough to keep me going back for more, whatever the result the previous week, whoever the opponents, whatever the weather – I was there like a bad penny. I enjoyed the highs of standing on Bunkers Hill (South Stand) whilst my heroes took a 2–1 lead into the interval against a well-known and respected Liverpool side.

I suffered the lows of being moved to the North – away – Stand to accommodate the Bradford City support in our end of the Stadium that followed their team to a promotion and in the process beating us that day. I endured the sadness in defeat to Darlington on the very last first-team game before moving to our new stadium.

I witnessed the comings and goings of chairmen, managers and players, shared champagne with Don Robinson (then chairman) who mingled amongst us to celebrate our promotion, receiving sweets from our sponsor Needlers (a Hull-based confectionery company) as some people walked around the pitch throwing them randomly into the crowd.

I faced the embarrassment of seeing our new mascot being paraded around the pitch when we were sponsored by Twydale (a local turkey-meat producer), as a guy in a massive wobbly turkey suit strutted around the pitch side to the joy of the visiting supporters. I have experienced, and in memory enjoyed, every possible emotion during my time watching the Tigers at Boothferry Park – a time never to be forgotten, and never to be repeated. Up the 'Ull.

Matthew Booth

AGGBOROUGH – KIDDERMINSTER HARRIERS

Name:
Aggborough

Highest attendance:
9,155, vs. Hereford United,
27 November 1948

First league match:
Kidderminster Harriers 2–0 Torquay United,
12 August 2000

Final league match:
Kidderminster Harriers 1–4 Grimsby Town,
30 April 2005

Memorable moment:
Kidderminster Harriers 1–1 Wolverhampton Wanderers,
3 January 2004
(FA Cup third round)

Current stadium:
Aggborough

The rather regally named Aggborough finally tasted League football at the second attempt in 2000. The stadium had been rejected five years previously owing to non-compliance with League regulations. But it has been home for Kidderminster Harriers since 1890, the club arriving from the nearby White Wickets cricket ground after switching codes from rugby.

Having staged various levels of non-League football around the Birmingham area, Aggborough remained largely untouched for many years, but it was the club's desire for League competition that saw work undertaken in 1989 where two covered stands behind each goal replaced the open terracing.

It was the beginning of a long-term redevelopment of the ground, but the Harriers' success came more quickly than expected. When promotion was achieved five years later, the ground was not complete owing to an extended FA Cup run and their League place was denied.

Harriers were not deterred, however, and that summer Aggborough's all-seater Main Stand was built, ensuring the ground met stringent League rules, but it was not yet complete. In 2003, while Harriers were a League club, they built the ground's focal point – an East Stand that could seat over 2,000 spectators and cost over £1 million, bringing the total redevelopment costs to over £2 million. Though the club was relegated back to the Conference in 2005, one thing is for sure; it only needs to rely on its form to bounce back.

MEMORIES

Being only a 40-minute car ride from the likes of West Bromwich Albion, Aston Villa and Wolves does tend to mean Harriers remains the 'second club' for many floating supporters, and can often mean the ground is only a quarter full these days, resulting in a lack of atmosphere.

Most visiting supporters would readily endorse the reputation of the catering at Aggborough as arguably the best in all of professional football. Balti Shepherd's pie anyone? Not to mention the truly legendary Aggborough Soup!

Both the stewards and home fans are a friendly enough lot, and crowd trouble is never encountered around the ground. The Harriers Arms attached to the ground is a busy and well-stocked watering hole to swap stories with the faithful.

Visitors should also note the occasional waft of pungent smoke across the pitch during the game from the steam trains on the adjacent Severn Valley Railway!

The existing 99-year lease was signed with the local council in the 1990s and so Kidderminster Harriers should safely remain in their current location for the foreseeable future.

Roy Davies

FILBERT STREET – LEICESTER CITY

Name:
Filbert Street

Highest attendance:
47,298, vs. Tottenham Hotspur,
18 February 1928

First league match:
Leicester City 4–2 Rotherham Town,
8 September 1894

Final league match:
Leicester City 2–1 Tottenham Hotspur,
11 May 2002

Memorable moment:
Leicester City 1–0 Liverpool,
7 August 1971 (FA Community Shield)

Current stadium:
The Walkers Stadium

Leicester City played at Filbert Street, nestled in the middle of densely-populated terraced housing, from 1891 until 2002 after having inhabited a number of different grounds in the first seven years of their history. For its early years Leicester Fosse were residents, but the club was wound up following World War I. Newly formed Leicester City took their place, though historians consider both clubs to be the same.

It was only after the Fosse era that the ground began to take shape. The Main Stand was opened in 1921, followed six years later by a double-decker South Stand, culminating in Filbert Street's record attendance in 1928. The old roof from the South Stand was transferred to the North, and the East Stand was covered after City reached their first ever FA Cup final in 1949.

The stadium remained largely untouched in the years to follow, save for seating being installed in the North, South and East Stands, bringing Filbert Street in line with the Taylor Report as the Foxes bounced between England's top two tiers. In 1994 a new Main Stand was constructed, known as the Carling Stand. This held nearly 10,000 spectators and cost a reported £5 million.

A sustained period of top-flight success in the late 1990s saw the club consider relocation, and just four years after the erection of the Carling Stand the club decided to relocate to a purpose-built stadium. This was named in conjunction with sponsors of the time, Walkers Crisps, while Filbert Street would become student accommodation for the nearby university.

Success was not immediate at their new home as City dropped to League Two for the first time in their history in 2008, climbing back the next year and advancing to the playoffs in 2010. Whether the move in 2002 had had an adverse effect on their fortunes was up for debate, but it's certain Premier League football would have filled the new ground and provided the resources to sustain a higher grade of football.

MEMORIES

'Filbo' was rich in character. The modern TV viewer's perception of the old place was based on the awful camera location above the old Wing Stand, which later made way for the Carling Stand in 1993. The view occasionally panned out allowing a full view of the old Kop below the wonderful old Double Decker stand, which Archie Leitch built in 1927, referred to locally as the 8th wonder of the world.

It was Martin O'Neil who said Filbo consisted of one fantastic stand, one adequate one, and the other two were Vauxhall Conference! New players were led into the ground backwards so their first impressions would be good ones.

But like generations of fans before him Martin also relished the Filbert Street night match. I loved night games at Filbo with so many memories to savour. Just what made it special could have been the walk to the ground through tightly knit streets of terraced houses and pubs. The floodlights were high and could have contributed allowing the night skies and distant buildings to be visible unlike the modern blinding brilliant lights that sit in the roof of new stands. The acoustics were phenomenal and City goals could be heard miles away.

As for the Walkers Stadium... well it's home now and what's really nice about it is that we walk the same way to the match and of course always have a quick sideways glance from the new Filbert Way over to this patch of land off Filbert Street where there is a student village at the end of Lineker Way! I swear you can see the ghosts of Rowley, Weller, Banks, Worthington, Dougan, Nish, Rodrigues, Cross, Sjoberg, Clarke and the rest.

Lots of special nights culminating in Athletico Madrid and also thrashing the arrogant Lee, Bell and Summerbee Man City with four goals in 20 minutes led by a rampant Frank Large. And of course Weller's first-half hat-trick to come back from 2–0 down to beat Liverpool are just a few priceless memories.

Chris Lewitt

MAINE ROAD – MANCHESTER CITY

Name:
Maine Road

Highest attendance:
84,569, vs. Stoke City,
3 March 1934

First league match:
Manchester City 2–1 Sheffield United,
25 August 1923

Final league match:
Manchester City 0–1 Southampton,
11 May 2003

Memorable moment:
Manchester City 4–1 Sheffield Wednesday,
1 May 1937
(Manchester City win First Division title)

Current stadium:
The City of Manchester Stadium (Eastlands)

Home to Manchester City before the club was a prince (though it was hardly a pauper), Maine Road was once the largest club ground in the country, breaking attendance records in both League and Cup games. City left a cramped and fire-damaged Hyde Road in 1923 to take up residence at a ground with an initial estimated capacity of 80–100,000, consisting of mainly terracing, and a Main Stand capable of holding 10,000 even though it didn't even extend the full length of the pitch.

The first improvements at Maine Road occurred either side of World War II when the Main Stand roofing was extended to cover the goal-side Platt Lane End, with benches installed after to give City the largest seating capacity in the country. The North Stand opposite was covered with a cantilever roof in the 1960s, shortly after. By the time the Main Stand roof was rebuilt in the 1980s, Maine Road had a distinctly hotchpotch appearance, with all the stands a different size and design.

This look was to be furthered with the redevelopment of the Platt Lane End in 1992 and the construction of the Kippax Street Stand opposite the Main Stand two years later to bring Maine Road in line with Britain's all-seater regulations. The three-tiered giant towered over the rest of the stadium and brought Maine Road's capacity to 35,000.

In its prime, Maine Road was used as an FA Cup semi-final venue, and when Manchester United shared the ground in the 1940s while Old Trafford was undergoing war damage repairs it was regularly registering 70–80,000 attendance figures. Whilst not having a small ground, City were still keen to relocate, and they capitalised on the Commonwealth Games coming to Manchester when they agreed a deal to occupy the 48,000-capacity City of Manchester Stadium in 2002, originally constructed for that occasion. They moved in the following year on a 250-year lease from Manchester City Council.

It was there that their fortunes skyrocketed, the take-over by Abu Dhabi billionaire Sheikh Mansour making them the richest club in the world. Time will tell if they become one of the leading clubs in the country, with a ground to match. Maine Road, the ground they left behind, was demolished in 2004.

MEMORIES

After 80 years, Manchester City retreated from Maine Road yesterday in defeat and disarray. But then some die harder than others. The point – and the glory – of this day at this ramshackle old ground was never going to be about any expectancy of success.

City had some wonderful moments here in Moss Side and the best of them were recreated poignantly when Nora Mercer, widow of Joe, Colin Bell and Malcolm Allison took the salute of a capacity crowd of 34,957, who had reassembled from various points of the world, including 10 young women from China who called themselves the Beijing Belles. Another wore a large lampshade over his head with the request that the last one out should turn off the lights. For him and his fellow fans a 1–0 defeat by Southampton was not so much a disaster as a final pinprick for bruised but still resilient souls.

Yes, of course, they will reappear in even greater numbers at the City of Manchester Stadium. They will come again with all their wounds and all those hopes, which you could see again yesterday, will never die.

The Independent, May 2003

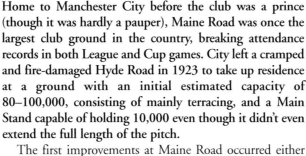

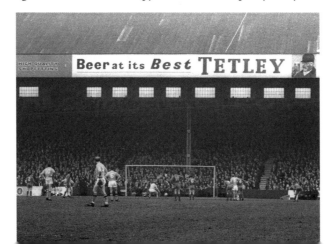

FIELD MILL – MANSFIELD TOWN

Name:
Field Mill

Highest attendance:
24,479, vs. Nottingham Forest,
10 January 1953

First league match:
Mansfield Town 3–2 Swindon,
29 August 1931

Final league match:
Mansfield 0–1 Rotherham United,
26 April 2008

Memorable moment:
Mansfield Town 3–0 West Ham United,
26 February 1969 (FA Cup fifth round)

Current stadium:
Field Mill

Field Mill is a site with large potential with ambitious owners. But that potential has only ever been partially realised owing to limited success on the field of play. Mansfield Town took over the ground from rivals Mansfield Mechanics in 1905, and was elected to the Football League 26 years later, where the club would stay for 77 years. The ground consisted of a Main Stand on the west side, with banking surrounding the pitch using ash from the nearby pits.

Prior to World War II the Bishop Street Stand was erected and took the status of Main Stand from its opposite neighbour, while the North Stand was covered in the 1950s.

The West Stand was rebuilt in 1959, when Mansfield emulated Accrington Stanley as they purchased a ready-made stand from Hurst Park Racecourse in London and had it transported and placed in the ground. This cost considerably more than forecast after additional transport costs, as was the case with Stanley's Peel Park. It was placed behind the existing West Stand, this being demolished in favour of a concrete paddock in front.

While aiming for promotion to the Second Division in the 1990s, plans were drawn up to redevelop Field Mill completely. In just three years, new stands were erected behind both goals and the West Stand rebuilt as a modern cantilever two-tier structure, so the capacity stands at 10,000. The Bishop Street Stand still remains but is seldom used, and plans for its redevelopment were put on hold as Mansfield dropped out of the League in 2008. If Field Mill's potential is to be fully realised, then Town need to fulfil its potential on the pitch first.

MEMORIES

My abiding memory of Field Mill before its redevelopment was seeing Leeds United come to play in the 1994–95 League Cup. The ground was nearly full to its then capacity of 10,000 and the Mansfield supporters invaded the pitch at the end of the game to celebrate their team's famous victory.

I also recall the first game in front of the redeveloped stands in 2000. The Quarry Lane end and North Stand were finished, but the West Stand was still being worked on. Watching games in this environment was a little strange, but Field Mill benefited greatly from the overhaul in the end.

The game itself was a 4–4 draw with Macclesfield. I also recall slightly before this period playing Nottingham Forest in the League Cup, a game that Mansfield won 1–0. This was when there were only two sides of the ground open and the atmosphere was rather muted given the well-fought victory over our local rivals.

I remember two distinct features about the pre-gentrification Field Mill – the clock on the North Stand and the old-fashioned scoreboard, which you had to buy a programme in order to get any use out of (i.e., each other fixture would be represented by a letter on the board, and the display simply had the letter and half-time score).

Paul Gelsthorpe

AYRESOME PARK – MIDDLESBROUGH

Name:
Ayresome Park

Highest attendance:
53,802, vs. Newcastle United,
27 December 1949

First league match:
Middlesbrough 2–3 Sunderland,
12 September 1903

Final league match:
Middlesbrough 2–1 Luton Town,
30 April 1995

Memorable moment:
North Korea 1–0 Italy, 19 July 1966
(World Cup group match)

Current stadium:
Riverside Stadium

Ayresome Park was Middlesbrough's sixth home in their 27-year history when they took up residence in 1903. The club had brought a stand from their former home at Linthorpe Road and deposited it on the South Side. The ground's only other covered stand at the time was the barrel-roofed North Stand opposite, with Ayresome capable of holding 40,000 fans.

The South Stand would be demolished and rebuilt in 1936, while shelter was created for the goal-side West End. The stadium became covered on all four sides in preparation for Ayresome being a host venue for the 1966 World Cup; the East Stand was covered and provided seating for 4,000, with additional seats installed in the North and South Stands. Despite Middlesbrough being a Third Division side at the time, it was a tribute to Ayresome Park that it was hosting such elite games.

But the improvements were in hindsight unnecessary; the ground had the lowest attendances of the tournament, and would go largely unchanged after. The bright red roofs on its four stands gave it a unique character, while its orderly layout, with the uncovered corners of the stadium neatly curving round to join the stands, was in keeping with football's elite.

Even so the stadium needed renovation in the 1990s, and the decision was to relocate to a brand new home in 1995, with Ayresome Park being sold off to housing developers. Middlesbrough signed off in fairytale fashion, defeating Luton Town to clinch the First Division Championship and gain promotion to the Premier League. In 2005 the club installed the old Ayresome gates in front of the Riverside Stadium, showing appreciation for their former residence that once figured on the world stage.

MEMORIES

The chicken run where all the fans that liked to dish abuse out was in the South Stand, singing came from the Holgate End where the EIO was invented – Bernie Slaven used to scale the fence after his goals too. For a friendly about 10,000 Celtic fans came down and invaded the pitch at half time. The police dogs were released and it was the best half-time show I've ever seen.

The famous 2–1 over Aston Villa while we were battling promotion from the old Second Division was televised on The Big Match Live. Mowbray had to have stitches in his head but came back on to score the winner with a diving header at the end.

Also Pears went off so Cooper went in goal and made the ladies swoon as he pulled his shorts down to tuck the GK jersey in and gave the North Stand an unobstructed view of his undercrackers. It should have been called Awesome Park.
Holgate67

Yeah I know it was falling to bits, and we now have a posh new stadium, but I really miss Ayresome too. Being in the Holgate on a Saturday afternoon was what my childhood was all about; the atmosphere was great.

I remember Arsenal fans coming in the Holgate (FA Cup, 1979) – and our fans absolutely hammering them. They were even shooting darts at each other (South Stand /Clive Road Corner), and the police had to put the goalmouth protectors up as a barrier between the two sets of fans.
Diggerman

THE DEN – MILLWALL

Name:

The Den

Highest attendance:

48,672, vs. Derby County,
20 February 1937

First league match:

Millwall 2–0 Bristol Rovers,
28 August 1920

Final league match:

Millwall 0–3 Bristol Rovers,
8 May 1993

Memorable moment:

Millwall 2–1 Norwich,
26 December 1966
(59th consecutive home game without defeat)

Current stadium:

The New Den

The Den was quite simply the most intimidating ground in the Football League. From Millwall's arrival in 1910 to their departure 83 years later, no team or supporter was keen to experience the frightening atmosphere and the 'Millwall roar', and the ground was shut owing to crowd trouble no less than five times by the FA.

The ground consisted of large terracing, with yellow crush barriers; seating was on part of the North Stand and the whole of the Main Stand, the original being destroyed in World War II. The north side had cover of the central section, but it only extended a third of the way toward the pitch, meaning fans had to congregate at the back to stay dry.

A police observation hut on site was a clear reminder of the threatening atmosphere inside the Den, and the majority of the ground being terracing gave the ground that old-school feel, but at the same time showed potential for disorder. The reluctance of the opposition to play at the Den was at its most evident when Millwall went on a two-and-a-half-year unbeaten run at home between 1964 and 1967.

When Millwall moved to the nearby New Den in 1993 it was the first stadium to comply with the Taylor Report, due to its being under construction when said report was published. It seemed as though the 'New London Stadium' – as it was first named, albeit briefly – would be a wholly different place from the Den. Nearly two decades on, however, the 'New' has been dropped from the ground's name and the ground is as intimidating as ever – proving, perhaps, that you can take the Lions out of the Den but you can't take the Den out of the Lions.

MEMORIES

'It may be a dump, but it's our dump.' Thus a Millwall fan on Radio 4 yesterday as he bade farewell to the Lions' dirty Den, their home for 80 years, in the knowledge that a new pile at nearby Senegal Fields was ready and waiting. But will the Lions become lambs in the Fields?

Well, on the pitch the players lost meekly enough to long-since relegated Bristol Rovers but spectators were not so sheepish, mounting a second-half pitch invasion, digging up the pitch and dismantling advertising hoardings before the final whistle, throwing sods at the directors' box and police, making off with at least four match balls and, after the match,

the goalposts. Mick McCarthy's side deserved a better send-off.

'The troublemakers were not passionate supporters, they were criminals disguised,' chief superintendent Ken Chapman said. All they have done is damage the reputation of Millwall Football Club. It's a tragedy for people who feel passionately about the club, because nobody has done more in the community than this club.

***The Independent,* May 1993**

CHRISTIE PARK – MORECAMBE

Name:
Christie Park

Highest attendance:
9,234, vs. Weymouth,
6 January 1962

First league match:
Morecambe 0–0 Barnet,
11 August 2007

Final league match:
Morecambe 2–1 Dagenham & Redbridge,
20 May 2010

Memorable moment:
Morecambe 3–1 Mansfield Town,
25 August 2007
(first win in the Football League)

Current stadium:
Morecambe Stadium

After battling their whole history, Morecambe finally delivered League football to Christie Park, albeit briefly, in 2007. It was a fitting farewell to the ground as, upon promotion to the League, plans were already in motion for a move to a new stadium at Westgate. Originally known as Roseberry Park, it was renamed by then president J. B. Christie and the name retained owing to the impact of his financial assistance in the club's early years.

Morecambe were formed in 1920, but it would be nearly 90 years before they would enter the League. Despite this, they had various successful cup runs, including a Lancaster Junior Cup final with Chorley FC that drew an impressive 30,000 spectators. Christie handed the ownership to Morecambe in 1927, shortly before his death, securing the immediate future of both club and stadium. The condition that, if Morecambe ever folded, the site should be used as a playground for the town's children was testament to the man's generosity.

The stadium's Main Stand sat on the halfway line, covered roughly half the pitch and had terracing in front of it. Morecambe's floodlight system caused obstructions, particularly with this stand, as two of the pylons stood in the sightlines of the Main Stand spectators. The uncovered terracing opposite was known as the 'Car Wash Terrace', owing to the vehicle cleaning service behind it. The covered terraces behind the north and south goals were for home and away supporters respectively, with the latter known as the Umbro Stand for sponsorship reasons.

The last game was a play-off semi-final against regular non-League foes Dagenham & Redbridge – and, though the 2-1 result was scant revenge for the 6-0 thrashing in the away leg, there were many cheers and tears when Dave Artell headed home the last ever goal at the stadium Morecambe had called home for nine decades.

Modern-day football and its financial situation meant that, when Morecambe announced their intentions to leave Christie Park, the ground would not have the idealistic use that its former owner envisaged. Instead it was sold to supermarket Sainsbury's to fund the move. The 6,000-capacity stadium's relationship with League Football was all too brief, and its name was a reminder of the man who kick-started Morecambe's journey to get there.

MEMORIES

When I first went to CP there was just a small wooden main stand, a small 'Scratchin Shed' at the South End, and two large slag heaps on the other two sides. After the 1961 Cup run to the third round, sadly losing at home to Weymouth, the present main stand was built followed a couple of years later by the now Umbro Stand.

The finest season of the era was 1967–68 when Morecambe won the treble of Lancashire Combination, the Lancashire Junior Cup and – for the only time by a non-League club – the Lancashire Senior Cup, beating a full-strength Burnley in the final.

1969 saw us move up the new Northern Premier League where we were to remain for many years. But in 1974 I went to Wembley to see us beat Dartford 2–1 to win the FA Trophy. Things were bad for years but the club has never been relegated in its history, and eventually at the 1994–95 season we won promotion to the Conference thanks to marines ground not being up to standard.

In 1997 Bobby Charlton opened our new 3,000 standing home end North Stand. In 2004 we lost in the play-offs to Dagenham & Redbridge at the semi-final stage after a heartbreaking penalty shootout.

But three years later under Sammy Mac we beat York in the semis and went to the new Wembley in 2007 where we beat Exeter 2–1 to gain our first promotion to League Two.

I personally will be very sad to leave Christie Park – it's been my other home for over 50 years, having played there as a junior – but the club needs to improve its income other than match days so we have to move.

I just hope the club remember Mr Christie when they name the new stadium because without him there would be no Morecambe FC.

Tony Wade

SOMERTON PARK – NEWPORT COUNTY

Name:

Somerton Park

Highest attendance:

24,268, vs. Cardiff City,

16 October 1937

First league match:

Newport County 0–1 Reading,

28 August 1920

Final league match:

Newport County 0–1 Rochdale,

7 May 1988

Memorable moment:

Newport County 0–1 Carl Zeiss Jena FC,

18 March 1981

(European Cup Winners' Cup quarter-final)

Current stadium:

Newport Stadium

Somerton Park was the site of both Newport County's greatest years and their worst – the period leading up to their demise in 1989. Throughout most of their tenure they were marginalised by their other tenants, both common stadium-sharers in the past in Britain; firstly the Cardiff Arms Park Greyhound Racing Company and, latterly, Newport Wasps speedway team. The club purchased the ground outright in 1980, but only enjoyed it for nine years before they dropped out of the League and folded.

Behind the goals were the Cromwell Road End and the Railway End, the latter nothing more than a shallow bank from which to watch the game. The Cromwell was covered and also terraced. Not much was done to the ground in its history, the main modifications occurring to accommodate Somerton's other sports; the pitch was moved to fit the dog-racing track, and the Main Stand was erected.

Division Two football was the highest level Somerton Park hosted, shortly before the outbreak of World War II, and again in 1980 for seven years, during which European football arrived at the stadium through the Welsh Cup. These were to be the precursor to tragedy, however, as County suffered successive relegations to drop out of the League, being wound up a year later after failing to complete their Conference fixtures.

The ground was reopened for newly formed Newport AFC to play there from 1992–93, but the club was moved on and Somerton Park was demolished for housing. From housing three sports clubs to housing families, it was now another ground reduced to mere memories. A re-formed County played away from Newport for several years before returning to the Spytty Park athletic stadium: as of 2010, they had regained Conference status.

MEMORIES

One part of the ground that everyone remembers is Paddy's Bar. It was at the top of the Stand which burnt down between the time we returned from exile and leaving the ground again to play at Gloucester.

Having played for the club's youth and reserves side, one thing that always sticks in my mind is how big the home dressing room was and the size of the bath in there and how good the pitch was to play on. We actually had a warm-up before a youth game in the changing room once! The bath was absolutely massive and could fit the whole team in there, but looking back now wasn't such a nice thing!

The Cromwell End was notorious and was the place to be if you were part of the casual scene or up for a bit of chanting/banter at the opposition fans who used to stand just across from us.

Too many games to say, but the usual derbies were always a bit of fun. Bristol City and Rovers, Swansea and of course Cardiff were always the ones that stand out for me along with the usual cup games.

Last but not least, the half-time cup of Bovril and pasty from the little brick buffet bars dotted around in the corners of the ground, bliss!

Amberarmy

As someone once wrote in a fanzine…it was a dump but it was our dump.

Giving the entire home end to the Everton lot in the FA Cup was a downer when they could have been caged in at the Railway End.

The Railway End! What was all that about? An open gravel slope behind bars. How that never turned into the perfect opportunity for stone throwing has always made

me wonder. But never mind; there was always the Cromwell End for launching items over the police to land in the away support.

Didn't we once get an award for the state of the pitch? Don't know who was responsible but some of the artwork and detail that went into the grass cutting was brilliant...shame about the team.

Toilets; now they were grim. Did any type of fresh water ever run down those walls?

There are so many memories of the County when they played at Somerton Park. My fan time started in about 1948; age is very cruel on the memory but I used to cycle to Somerton and on one occasion made myself sick with the effort to get to the match on time. Some kindly chap got me taken to the dressing room and as

I lay on the bench I was passed by the whole team who were about to play. I can't recall the name of the opposition but I'll never forget that experience.

There were the times that I spent with my family on the Railway End embankment. Yes there was a lot of barracking and general joviality, but light-hearted banter and very funny. Then there were the times of the local derbies between Cardiff and Merthyr Tydfil when the great John Charles played for them. I have watched Tommy Lawton play and the one and only Sir Stanley Matthews. But this is too far back now and remains an image in my mind.

Brian Gough

COUNTY GROUND – NORTHAMPTON TOWN

Name:
County Ground
Highest attendance:
24,523, vs. Fulham,
23 April 1966
First league match:
Northampton Town 4–1 Grimsby,
4 September 1920
Final league match:
Northampton Town 0–1 Mansfield Town,
11 October 1994
Memorable moment:
Northampton Town 3–0 Hull City,
24 May 1963
(Northampton win Third Division title)
Current stadium:
Sixfields Stadium

The County Ground was primarily a venue for cricket, but it witnessed the incredible ascent of Northampton Town Football Club and its equally astounding descent. In a 12-year period between 1958 and 1970, Town rose from the Fourth Division all the way to the summit of English football, only to fall back down again.

The Cobblers had played at the County Ground since their formation in 1897, and it was for a time the only three-sided football ground in the League owing to the size of the cricket pitch. The home fans congregated in the Hotel End terrace that was covered after World War II. Opposite was the Spion Kop, a deceptively titled uncovered terrace much smaller than its name suggested

The Main Stand was built in 1924 after the previous one was destroyed by fire, but it was another fire – Bradford City's at Valley Parade in 1985 – that caused the Main Stand to be deemed unsafe and demolished, like many other wooden structures across the country. The small stand built to replace it was mockingly dubbed the 'Meccano Stand' owing to its resemblance to the model construction kit.

Throughout their time at the County Ground, Northampton were always considered secondary to the cricket club, so they moved to their new 7,600-capacity Sixfields Stadium, complete with four sides, midway though the 1994–95 campaign, leaving the cricketers in situ.

At the end of their last full season at the County Ground, Town finished bottom of the Football League, saved from relegation only by Kidderminster's Aggborough Stadium failing to meet League criteria. Considering their freefall from 1966 to 1970, Northampton would be hoping for a slightly quieter life at their new home, and so far that has been granted.

MEMORIES

The Hotel End was not just an end; it was a living thing to any Cobblers supporters who happened to have the good fortune to be part of it. It breathed, it sighed, it moaned and it roared; all of this it did in unison.

It was where I cut my teeth as a football supporter. It will always be my favourite place on earth. They may have taken it from me, but they can never take it out of me. I would have defended that place with my life – and on occasions we fought for it.

You can call me a dinosaur all you like. I wouldn't raise a finger to keep my place at Sixfields, but the Hotel End belonged to me and anybody else who loved the Cobblers. It belonged to the supporters. It was our piece of England.
Terryfenwickatemyhamster

You didn't need thousands in there to get up an atmosphere; you didn't need to be a 'face' to be accepted. You had a real feel of camaraderie. You had your regular chant leaders that the rest happily joined in with. You didn't feel a prat if you tried to start a song, because 99 times out of 100 you would always get someone to join in!

The stand itself had an eerie echo, which gave us many a laugh when you got someone with a booming voice having a moan! On the whole you very quickly knew your own supporters and this was handy on many an occasion when the away fans infiltrated our stand! A few signals and 'runs' between the two exit stairs and virtually everyone knew the score and where the infiltrators were!

You could choose who you stood with and where in the stand. You felt at times that you were on the pitch with the players, and indeed, you almost were if you got caught up with 'knock kneed chicken' or when we scored a goal!

In short, happy, brilliant memories, many good friends made, in a place that I just wish could have been moved to Sixfields!
Moll!

MANOR GROUND – OXFORD UNITED

Name:
Manor Ground

Highest attendance:
22,730, vs. Preston North End,
29 February 1964

First league match:
Oxford United 2–1 Lincoln City,
22 August 1962

Final league match:
Oxford United 1-1 Port Vale,
1 May 2001

Memorable moment:
Oxford United 2–1 Aston Villa,
12 March 1986
(League Cup semi-final, second leg)

Current stadium:
Kassam Stadium

For nearly half its history, the Manor Ground was home to Headington United, who became Oxford United in 1960, shortly before heading into the Football League in 1962, replacing Accrington Stanley. United had moved to the Manor Ground from Britannia Field in 1925 with the city's cricket, tennis and bowls clubs. Twenty-five years later and football was the only sport being played at the stadium.

The first stand to be built was the Manor Club, nestled in the corner between where the Main Stand and the uncovered, northerly sloping terracing of the Cuckoo Lane End would later be. The former was next to be built in anticipation of League football in 1957. It duly arrived in 1962 and six years later Oxford found themselves in Division Two.

Opposite was the Osler Road Terrace, essentially three separate stands, with each roof section slightly higher than the other. Behind the east goal was the London Road End, simple terracing under a corrugated iron roof.

United enjoyed perhaps their best success at the Manor Ground in the 1980s as they competed in the First Division and even won the League Cup in 1986, the prospect of European football thwarted by the ban on English clubs after the Heysel disaster. But as time moved on and sterner safety regulations were imposed on football grounds in Britain, the idyllic Manor Ground was becoming increasingly outdated and it became clear a move would soon be on the cards.

The club's financial situation meant construction of a new stadium was halted, before millionaire Firoz Kassam bought the club and set about clearing their debts. Oxford left the Manor Ground in 2001 to their new Kassam Stadium, named after the man who got them there, and the Manor was demolished and replaced with a hospital, a nice change from the popular option of a retail park.

Oxford United would have mixed fortunes at their new home. Having said goodbye to the Manor by being relegated to the Third Division, they dropped out of the Football League five years later in 2006, only to return via the Conference play-offs in 2010.

MEMORIES

Memories? 4–0 versus Barnsley to get us into the top flight, watched from the ramshackle Cuckoo Lane End, because they opened half of it up to us. The second reply against Man U in 1984, looping header...get in! Ian Botham turning out for Scunthorpe (can't remember anything of his performance, though). First ever pay-per-view game 0–0 bore draw against the Mackems, better than the 7–0 up there though – lordy.
Its_M

The London Road Stand was without doubt the most intimidating terrace in world football. Whether it was the 'You're gonna get your heads kicked in' chant (Joe Pasquale style) that they persisted with 20 years after everyone else had stopped using it, the inaccurate coin throwing at Steve Mildenhall when on the way to losing the final ever derby game at the famous old stadium, or the ones who ran on the pitch against Chelsea but got nicked and banned before they came anywhere near reaching the opposition fans, it still sends a chill down the spine, even now.

They certainly made sure that no one ever enjoyed their trip to Oxford.
Leroy

THE OLD RECREATION GROUND – PORT VALE

Name:
The Old Recreation Ground

Highest attendance:
22,993, vs. Stoke City,
6 March 1920

First league match:
Port Vale 0–1 Tottenham Hotspur,
27 October 1919

Final league match:
Port Vale 0–1 Aldershot Town,
22 April 1950

Memorable moment:
Port Vale 5–2 Lincoln City,
19 April 1930
(start of a five-match winning streak that secured
Third Division North title)

Current stadium:
Vale Park

The Old Recreation Ground was an example of the importance of a club owning its own stadium. Port Vale moved there in 1913 and rented it from the council. It was their sixth home since their formation in 1876, having played on various fields in the area including waste ground. It was here Port Vale would adopt their club colours of black and white and achieve some of their biggest success.

Vale's first League game at the stadium was in October 1919 after returning for a third attempt at League football. They replaced disgraced Leeds City after that club was ejected from the League for making illegal payments, Port Vale taking over the remaining fixtures. The Valiants went on to achieve their highest ever League position, fifth in the Second Division, in 1931, something they have yet to equal at Vale Park.

The club bought the ground in 1927 after a period of stability in the League, but mounting debts saw them sell their prized asset back to the council 16 years later – a move that would take the club's future out of its own hands. Port Vale's stay at The Old Recreation Ground was all too brief, as the city council decided to construct a giant indoor shopping centre on the land, forcing them to look elsewhere.

Grand plans were drawn up for the 'Wembley of the North', but the new stadium fell short of this lofty advertisement owing to the club's financial position and the lack of material following World War II. On the site of Vale's old home now stands the multi-storey car park for the Potteries Shopping Centre. The stadium is now of a different generation of Vale fans, but it was the site where the foundations were laid for the club's history.

MEMORIES

The Old Rec was where a football ground ought to be, right in the centre of things. When the crowd roared it echoed round the town and the temptation was irresistible. I have it on good authority that men gave their wives a peck on the cheek in the middle of shopping and raced off to the match.

I won't dwell on supporters likening their dedication to a religious experience. But at the Old Rec I stood with old men who spoke with reverence of the Port Vale war cry, which sadly I never heard. It must have died out by the late 1940s.

However, the ground did have a chap who regularly waited for a quiet moment in play before bellowing 'Have no bluddy mercy, Vale', particularly if Vale were losing.

Another long-lost sound which sticks in my mind is that of the heavy ball when a sturdy full-back like Bob Purcell thumped it hard. It was like a gunshot.

My late father's favourite spot at the Old Rec was the Bryan Street Paddock. I could never understand why. It was like standing in a deep moat. You had a great view of the players' boots but little else. The paddock was also close to the touchline and a player sometimes fell off the pitch into the crowd. Nobody worried. They just threw him back.

I preferred the terraces on the opposite side, where we were equally close to the action. Indeed, Vale's winger Mick Hulligan had a running conversation with those at the front.
John Abberly

WHITE CITY STADIUM (1930–31, 1962–63) – QPR

Name:
White City Stadium

Highest attendance:
41,097, vs. Leeds United,
9 January 1932

First league match:
QPR 0–3 Bournemouth,
5 September 1931

Final league match:
QPR 1–3 Coventry City,
22 May 1963

Memorable moment:
France 1–1 Mexico,
13 July 1966
(World Cup group match)

Current stadium:
Loftus Road

Queens Park Rangers have had the most homes of any Football League club, but aside from their main abode of Loftus Road the club spent two brief spells at the nearby White City Stadium in 1931–33 and again 30 years later in 1962–63. The multi-purpose athletics venue was built in less than a year for the 1908 Olympic Games in London and was somewhat pretentiously titled the Great Stadium. It could hold 130,000 spectators, with nearly 70,000 of those seating – a first at the time.

Having settled at Loftus Road in 1917 after a nomadic early existence, the club began to build some impressive attendances. The move to the much bigger White City Stadium at the other end of South Africa Road was undertaken in 1931, Loftus Road being kept for reserve team games with plans to sell it at a later date.

When they arrived at White City for their first spell, the stadium's Olympian standing was somewhat diminished and it was primarily used for greyhound racing.

The stadium was originally uncovered for the most part, with just two roofs opposite each other midway up the field. The field itself was big enough to include the vast amount of sports it catered for at the Olympics and after. There was even an outdoor swimming pool on one side.

The huge oval arena was just too big for QPR's support; attendances didn't rise as predicted, the club couldn't fill a fifth of the stadium for League contests and, with the death of the club's chairman, Rangers found themselves in financial trouble. They were saved by the fact that Loftus Road hadn't been sold as planned.

QPR's second spell at White City in the 1960s was much shorter – only half a season – and was at the suggestion of manager Alec Stock; a proposed ground share with Fulham had been mooted, but never occurred. The stadium hosted a group match between France and Mexico in the 1966 World Cup after greyhound racing precluded the use of Wembley.

White City Stadium survived through various uses including speedway until 1985, when it was demolished and replaced with BBC buildings. QPR returned to Loftus Road, and, when they were taken over in 2007 by racing mogul and millionaire Flavio Briatore, thoughts turned to a time when the club could fill a stadium the size of White City.

MEMORIES

The old White City Stadium in London. Built for the 1908 Olympic Games, it later hosted world-class athletics, top-flight cycling, football (QPR had spells there while Loftus Road was out of commission) and even – once Wembley refused to cancel a scheduled greyhound racing meeting – the 1966 World Cup match between France and Uruguay. In 1986, this Alhambra of British sporting and cultural greatness was unceremoniously bulldozed to make way for an eyesore cell block that now houses the senior management of the BBC.
The Times, **March 2007**

ELM PARK – READING

Name:
Elm Park

Highest attendance:
33,042, vs. Brentford,
19 February 1927

First league match:
Reading 1–2 Gillingham,
1 September 1920

Final league match:
Reading 0–1 Norwich,
3 May 1998

Memorable moment:
Reading 2–0 Brighton & Hove Albion,
30 April 1994
(Reading win Second Division title)

Current stadium:
Madejski Stadium

When Reading moved to Elm Park in 1896 they had already been in existence for 25 years, unusual for a team in the South. They had spells at the Reading Recreation Ground and Reading Cricket Ground, then latterly Coley Park and Caversham Cricket Ground. Elm Park was to be Reading's first League home, however, when they were elected in 1920.

The stadium remained largely unchanged for the duration of its existence. Upon Reading's arrival there was cover on half the Norfolk Road Stand, this wrapping round to cover half the Town End; however, it was short-lived as it fell victim to the elements. It was swiftly replaced by a Main Stand that would stay in place until the club left; a covered terrace running the length of the Norfolk Road side of the pitch, with seats later installed, would be the only stand in the stadium that allowed spectators to sit.

After World War II shelter was erected on the opposite Tilehurst Terrace, covering the centre section, the flanks quickly following at the turn of the 1950s. Behind the goals were the uncovered Tilehurst End for the home fans and the Town End for the visitors.

After challenging in the First Division in the 1990s, the club believed the Premier League was attainable, so the club moved to a new stadium in time for the 1998–99 season, with Elm Park succumbing to housing. The 24,000-capacity Madejski Stadium, named after chairman John Madejski, was primed for top-flight football, but unfortunately the Royals' last season at Elm Park resulted in relegation to the Second Division; it would be eight years before they would reach the Promised Land.

MEMORIES

Scalding Hot Bovril in paper cups. tannoy that sounded like a strangled parrot and 'Dancing Queen' by Abba played every week.

Dodging puddles in the loos! Legendary groundsman Gordon Neate killing the pitch by spreading weed killer instead of fertiliser.

The horror on the faces of the 'big' clubs' away fans when they saw the facilities.

Feeling embarrassed for the players acknowledging the fans in games at a near-empty Elm Park in the early 1980s.

A full Elm Park in the late 1980s and 90s almost taking off under the floodlights when we scored – very tight ground.

Four generations of my family standing frozen/boiling side by side at the Town End and the then Tilehurst End.

5' 7" keeper Steve Death who must have had springs in his boots.

Feeling annoyed that I had just missed out on seeing Robin Friday play for the club.
Ginger_Blitz

My first memories of Elm Park are of watching the reserves playing Orient on a nice spring evening in about 1978. My father's friend lived behind the Town End where there was a car park. The stadium was really run-down, and uncared-for, the atmosphere typified by a dumped mattress that took residence in the car park. We entered through a small turnstile in Norfolk Road and, climbing the wooden steps, sat in the stand. I always found the ground to be unpretentious and scruffy. The seats would not stay up as the stand had sunk at the front.

On the opposite side stood the South Bank, the big terrace, which held about 4,000. The crowd in this stand generally used to dictate the atmosphere on match days. I always stood on this terrace during the cold weather as we felt warmer all huddled together. I remember having to pick our standing position carefully – stand in the wrong place and you ended up smelling the toilets coupled with a scent of burgers and overcooked onions!

During the later years the club built a social club behind the South Bank, a two-storey building that seemed too small for its purpose. The manager of the social club at that time was ex-player Mick Kearney and the players used to have their pre-match meal upstairs during the Mark McGhee era. During the warmer months, at the beginning and end of the season I used to like to stand at the top of the Tilehurst Road End, the most run-down part of the stadium. The exit gates were rusty,

battered corrugated iron and the walls were tall, poorly plastered and dirty. The atmosphere in that part of the ground always felt muted as the noisy end of the South Bank seemed so far away.

Elm Park was an antiquated, tiny, unforgiving ground but it did have character and atmosphere. I loved it because it never changed in all the years I attended. To the away fans and the outsiders it was seen as a dump. The Madejski Stadium is a wonderful arena to watch football – every seat in the ground is the best one there for its own individual reasons – but part of my love for Reading FC died when the club moved. It doesn't feel the same.
Paul Jameson

MILLMOOR – ROTHERHAM UNITED

Name:
Millmoor

Highest attendance:
25,170, vs. Sheffield United,
13 December 1952

First league match:
Rotherham County 2–0 Nottingham Forest,
30 August 1919

Final league match:
Rotherham United 1–0 Barnet,
3 May 2008

Memorable moment:
Rotherham 2–0 Aston Villa,
22 August 1961
(League Cup final, first leg)

Current stadium:
Don Valley Stadium

The result of a merger between neighbouring Rotherham Town and Rotherham County, United played at the latter's home of Millmoor after uniting in 1925, and assumed County's League position and fixtures. Far from idyllic, Millmoor was surrounded by scrapyards and a dilapidated cinema, and as such made for a cramped environment, with everyone residing and working on top of one another.

An incarnation of the Main Stand was built in the late 1920s, with partial covering also erected over the Millmoor Lane side opposite. Either end behind the goals were the Railway and Tivoli End terraces, the latter named after the rustic cinema situated behind it. The Railway End was covered in 1957, its counterpart opposite 11 years later. In between times a gymnasium was built next to the Main Stand on the Railway End side, another cosy neighbour for Rotherham to share with.

In 1982 another section of the Millmoor Lane Stand was covered, towards the Railway End again, giving the flanks of the pitch a hotchpotch appearance. Towards the end of Rotherham's time at Millmoor the facilities were deemed sub-standard for both supporters and opposing teams, with West Ham players refusing to change in the Millmoor dressing rooms in 2001. The lack of comfort proved to be to Rotherham's advantage that day, as they defeated the Hammers.

Things quickly took a turn for the worse for both United and Millmoor, as the team suffered two relegations and fell from the second tier to the basement in just three seasons. Financial difficulties and subsequent points deductions helped the process along.

In 2008, after failing to complete a deal for Millmoor with the Booth family who owned it, Rotherham decided to move to the Don Valley Stadium in Sheffield, sharing with Sheffield Eagles Rugby League club and City of Sheffield Athletics Club, until they could complete a new stadium in Rotherham, leaving their old home in disuse. Millers fans hoped for a brighter future in a home of their own, this optimism encouraged by a bright 2009-10 season that saw them reach the League Two play-off final.

MEMORIES

A memory that particularly sticks out is the 4–4 home draw with Norwich City in the Championship. Rotherham had taken the lead but ended up going in at half time 3–2 down; they had won and scored a very, very controversial penalty just before the break which eventually led to the half-time dismissal of (player) Guy Branston, and (manager) Ronnie Moore was sent to the stands.

Not long after the break Martin Butler completed his perfect hat-trick, a right foot, left foot and header to level things. The atmosphere was terrific at this point but when John Mullin pounced to put us 4–3 up, the whole ground was on its feet, it was electric.

The game eventually ended 4–4 with the Canaries grabbing an equaliser in the last few moments, but it was a fantastic game and an amazing atmosphere that day. The overall attendance was around 7,500 with around 2,300 from Norwich as it was the year they went on to be promoted to the Premiership.

Another that springs to mind was the 1–0 win against Leeds United. We had started the season poorly and hadn't won in 17 games – hence our League position, rooted to the bottom of the Championship. Leeds had just been relegated from the Premier League and turned up at Millmoor huge favourites and I would imagine feeling confident of taking the points.

The crowd was well up for it, Leeds had 2,500 in and the whole feeling of a Yorkshire derby had kicked in well before kick-off. The game saw both teams create and waste a host of chances, it was looking like a 0–0 draw was in the making, but around 78 minutes in Martin McIntosh smashed in a close-range effort to put us 1–0 up.

The Leeds fans were silenced, Millmoor was bouncing and the world could see it, as it was live on Sky Sports. After the goal the Millers found confidence and began toying with the 'Mighty' Leeds, the crowd cheering each pass and the fact that we hadn't won in the 17 previous games, and given Leeds's huge history, it was a sweet, sweet last 15 minutes. It finished 1–0 and, although we went on to be relegated, that match will never be forgotten.

I miss Millmoor, the close-to-pitch experience, the atmosphere when the Tivoli End was at its best, the sense of history written in the old walls, turnstiles, etc, the ticket office in a Portakabin gave that small club doing its temporary best feeling. It will never be forgotten and long may it stand but now it is on to a bigger and better future in a bigger and better new stadium when built.

Keiren Smith

Lost League Football Grounds | 89

NENE PARK – RUSHDEN & DIAMONDS

Name:
Nene Park

Highest attendance:
6,431, vs. Leeds United,
2 January 1999

First league match:
Rushden & Diamonds 0–0 Lincoln City,
16 August 2001

Final league match:
Rushden & Diamonds 1–2 Barnet,
6 May 2006

Memorable moment:
Rushden & Diamonds 1–1 Hartlepool United,
3 May 2003
(Rushden & Diamonds win League Two title)

Current stadium:
Nene Park

Despite the bland name for a particularly adventurously titled club, Nene Park is rather idyllically situated on the banks of the River Nene. The stadium pre-dates its incumbents whose formation in 1992 was the result of a merger between Rushden Town and Irthlingborough Diamonds. The stadium was acquired by the Diamonds from the water board in 1969, many years before the union.

The whole stadium was systematically redeveloped after the merger, beginning in 1993 with the North Stand. When completed it could seat 1,000 spectators. The opposite South Stand quickly followed in 1994 to complete the flanking of the pitch. In addition, the newly built Diamond Centre housed everything from the players' and staff dressing rooms, to conference rooms and a restaurant. The ground was looking ready for League football.

The Peter DeBanke Terrace – named after a popular ex-supporter – was next to be completed behind the west goal, a simple covered terrace that nevertheless was in keeping with its all-seated neighbours. Behind the opposite goal on the east side would be the focal point of the new Nene Park, the Airwair Stand completed in 1997. Initially roofless in order to be completed and eligible for League status, the arched roof added later would be the highlight of the stadium, which now held nearly 6,500.

Equipped with the most modern ground in non-League football, it was no surprise when Nene Park eventually hosted League competition in 2001. Before long it was witnessing a further promotion as the Diamonds soared to League One. But things quickly went wrong for the club, and two rapid relegations meant their five-year stay in the Football League had come to an end.

MEMORIES

The Division Three championship trophy shone like diamonds as Rushden claimed the title amidst wild scenes of celebration at Nene Park.

Paul Hall's 16th goal of the season was as sweet as you like for Rushden who were hell bent on going up in style – as champions. They endured a nerve-wracking last few minutes after Chris Westwood equalised, but managed to hang on.

It was remarkable that Diamonds went up as champions as they were 14 points behind Hartlepool until the beginning of March. But when they hit the slippery slope, Rushden seized the opportunity to close the gap and claim top spot after a 10-match unbeaten run.

Rushden boss Brian Talbot said: 'This is a great achievement for this football club and a credit to everyone who has played their part. Last year we were devastated after losing in the play-off final, and we called the players together afterwards and all agreed that we didn't want to go through that disappointment again.

'The players should take great credit for the run they have put together over the last two months. We were miles behind Hartlepool but we kept plugging away, and every time we picked up three points they seemed to be losing and we managed to close the gap.

'Hopefully I can keep the majority of what is a very good squad together next season, but I'm only the manager and that sort of thing is out of my hands.

'It will be tough next season because we don't have massive resources, but let's not worry about the future – let's savour this moment of success.'

Sunday Mirror, May 2003

McCAIN STADIUM – SCARBOROUGH

Name:
McCain Stadium

Highest attendance:
11,162, vs. Luton Town,
FA Cup, 8 January 1938

First league match:
Scarborough 2–2 Wolverhampton Wanderers,
15 August 1987

Final league match:
Scarborough 1–1 Peterborough
United, 8 May 1999.

Memorable moment:
Scarborough 3–2 Chelsea,
4 October 1989
(League Cup second round)

Current stadium:
N/A

Scarborough FC's demise was intertwined with its home of 109 years. An old covenant preventing the site of the McCain Stadium from being used for anything other than sporting activities, ultimately ended the club's dreams of selling it to pay off their debts and secure a new stadium elsewhere. The result was Scarborough FC being wound up in the courts in 2007.

The club arrived in 1898 after leaving the ground they shared with the cricket club; their new home was originally the Athletics Ground. A sponsorship deal with food giants McCain in 1988 changed that, and instead of being ashamed of the deal – indicative of the modern game – fans embraced it, ironically naming their home the 'Theatre of Chips'.

In 1999 Scarborough and the McCain Stadium lost League status. While everyone remembers goalkeeper Jimmy Glass's goal that kept Carlisle in the League, many forget the scenes at the McCain; hundreds of Scarborough fans already on the pitch in premature celebration then sat down in utter dejection as they realised their fate.

Languishing in non-League was difficult for the club that enjoyed its 12-year stay among the country's top clubs, and with debts mounting it decided to sell the Stadium in 2006 to stave off the debt collectors and pay for a new 4,000-seater home nearby.

Unfortunately, a feature of a bygone era prevented this; a covenant in place from the ground's creation prevented anything other than sport on the site. Ironically for the club this effectively ended its existence, and the McCain has fallen into disrepair. In December 2008 the council finally purchased the ground from the liquidators and Scarborough Athletic, who play out of town in Bridlington with gates of less than 500, expressed an interest in moving back to the stadium.

MEMORIES

For someone like myself who enjoyed so many memories of playing at that stadium it is an absolute disgrace to see how it is being treated.

A lot of good players have played there over the years and when we got promoted into the Football League under Neil Warnock it was one of the biggest moments of my career. The atmosphere at the ground was excellent and there was a hardcore of fans that always cheered us on.

I am aware that Scarborough Athletic are looking for somewhere to play and it would be great to be able to have football back at the ground.

Kevin Blackwell, quoted in Scarborough Evening News, July 2008

A fog-bound FA Cup Tie against Arsenal in 1993...and only losing 1–0 to the Gunners, all owing to Boro's excellent football and nothing at all to do with the fact that the players couldn't see the ball!

Karl Taylor

OLD SHOW GROUND – SCUNTHORPE UNITED

Name:

Old Show Ground

Highest attendance:

23,935, vs. Portsmouth,

30 January 1954

First league match:

Scunthorpe United 0–0 Shrewsbury Town,

19 August 1950

Final league match:

Scunthorpe United 1–1 Torquay United,

18 May 1988

Memorable moment:

Scunthorpe United 3–1 Carlisle United,

1 May 1958

(Scunthorpe lift the Third Division North title)

Current stadium:

Glanford Park

Scunthorpe United could be known as leading innovators of the British football stadium scene. During their time at the Old Show Ground they were the first team to implement the use of a cantilevered roof, producing an unobstructed view under cover for the spectator. On leaving for Glanford Park in 1988, they became the first team to relocate to a new purpose-built home since Southend United moved to Roots Hall over 30 years earlier. Countless teams would follow their lead.

The club had played there from their formation in 1899, and later merged with North Lindsey United, dropping Lindsey from their title in 1958. The Main Stand that survived until the ground's demolition was constructed in 1925, after its previous incarnation was gutted by fire. The Fox Street Terrace was covered in 1938, with its opposite number, the Doncaster Road End terrace, covered 16 years later.

When the wooden roof of the East Stand also succumbed to fire in 1957, it was replaced by Britain's first cantilevered roof, appropriately built by the Irons' local United Steel Structural Company four years before Sheffield Wednesday built one at Hillsborough. The stand sat alongside the middle of the pitch with terracing either side, like the Main Stand opposite.

After the disaster at Valley Parade, and with new safety regulations to meet, United made the decision to sell the Old Show Ground to the Sainsbury's supermarket chain and move to a new purpose-built but significantly smaller stadium. Scunthorpe said goodbye to the ground by crashing out of the play-offs to Torquay United, but recent success on the pitch has brought the crowds flocking to Glanford Park to watch Championship football. The Old Show Ground they left behind is now a retail park.

MEMORIES

Take a trip with me around the shabby, yet rewarding, sprawl that was the Old Show Ground. The home of Scunthorpe United during their glory days of the 1950s and less glorious dark ages of the early '70s, it was looking its age for a long time before Graham Pearson decided to 'clear our debts' by laying it to waste.

I used to enter, with my Dad, in the late 1960s, behind the magnificent cantilever East Stand. All-seated apart from the paddock at the front, this stand was a fine place from which to watch the dire fare on offer. It was divided into three sections vertically, the middle section being proper seats, the outer sections being benches. There was a tunnel in the paddock below leading to where the lawnmowers, etc, were kept under the stand. This was also where the players would train in bad weather. Walking from the East Stand paddock towards the Donny Road end there was a section of uncovered terracing, about 12 steps deep. Behind the terrace was a muck and stone bank leading down to the toilets and an eight-foot wall topped with broken glass that was a poor deterrent to the penniless youth of the day! Further on were the turnstiles and big double exit gates that were opened not long after half time for dishevelled urchins to gain entrance and disenchanted old men to escape. Up the slope from the turnstile was the floodlight on its solid concrete base, which was often clambered up by the aforementioned free-wheelers.

Now we come to the legendary Donny Road end. In truth it was a dark and damp shed but it was where we learned our football-supporting skills. It could probably hold about 9,000, not particularly comfortably. Behind the stand were the vilest toilets in the ground and the second easiest point of free entry (the easiest being behind the Fox Street End). The petrol station had a handy, scaleable fence that backed onto the toilet roof and there was often a queue of parka-clad rogues and vagabonds waiting to snag their wrist-tied silk scarves on the barbed wire. At the top of the terrace was a snack bar, which was the setting for a particularly amusing food fight when Sheffield United fans strolled across the pitch and 'took' the Donny Road. The singers stood to the left of the snack bar and the age groups could be differentiated by their relative positions on the terracing of the 'kop'.

At half-time, in the good old days, if United were kicking towards the Fox Street in the second-half, the majority of the Donny Road would head round behind the West Stand to the other end. This entailed walking down to a fence that was supposed to keep the hoi polloi apart from the more refined customer in the Hendy Ave paddock. A coffin-dodger who had neither the time nor the inclination to stop anyone from going through manned a gate in the fence. At the top of the fence, on the Donny Road side, was a programme shop that was frequented by the anoraked dullards among us. On passing through the gate the older of our number could make their way through to the old Henderson Avenue Club, which formed part of the ground, along with a betting shop.

The West Stand was the oldest part of the ground and the dearest. Up in the seats it was also the place with the worst view. There were at least half a dozen pillars blocking the view of the slumbering directors and, during night matches, it was the darkest place on earth. At the front of the old stand was another, deeper, paddock which was a meeting place for the 'Ashman Out' brigade who stood directly behind the dug-out giving dear old Ron a hearty welcome every game. The paddock on the other side of the players' tunnel was where the 'Lads' would stand for the Grimsby, Lincoln, Donny, etc, games. It was also the best vantage point for seeing the skies light up during night matches. After walking round the back of the West Stand you had the choice of going into this paddock or walking down a slag track to the Fox Street terrace.

Above the terrace leading to the Fox Street was the late, lamented 1500 Club where miserable old sods could be seen staring out of tear-stained windows at the shabby offerings below. The Fox Street End was nearly identical to the Donny Road but, from here, the ground looked completely different. You could see a definite slope in the pitch from West to East

and the Donny Road, obviously, always looked fuller. Behind the Fox Street was the main access point for rob-dogs; Dyas Motors had a scruffy mesh fence that was ripped apart in many places and there was always a lack of stewards, away we went!

The Fox Street End was the scene of two of my abiding memories of the OSG; it was full of Grimsby fans, many in white boiler suits in the style of Clockwork Orange, and one of my mates was the last ever person arrested on the OSG during the last ever game versus Torquay for stealing a Torquay flag and running back with it towards the Donny Road.

Mik Henry

Well the reason I support Scunthorpe is due to going to the Old Show Ground. My dad – a Preston fan – took me to see his team play Scunthorpe in 1986. I remember going with my younger brother and sister too; living in Doncaster I guess it wasn't far for us to travel.

I think he took us there in the hope we'd all go home Preston

fans. I remember standing behind the goal and some bloke asking us to hold his Union Jack emblazoned with PNE in place.

Well, that day changed my life and my dad's hopes and wishes. Scunthorpe won 4–0; I was a boy of 10 and had just seen a team score four goals – what else was I to do?

From that day on my heart was with Scunthorpe United; I've supported them ever since up and down the country.
Gareth Holden

GAY MEADOW – SHREWSBURY TOWN

Name:
Gay Meadow

Highest attendance:
18,917, vs. Walsall,
26 April 1961

First league match:
Shrewsbury Town 2–1 Wrexham,
21 August 1950

Final league match:
Shrewsbury Town 0–0 MK Dons,
14 May 2007

Memorable moment:
Shrewsbury 4–1 Exeter City,
17 May 1979
(Shrewsbury win Third Division title)

Current stadium:
The New Meadow

Gay Meadow, its very name itself indicative of a golden age, was every bit as picturesque as its named suggested. Shrewsbury Town moved to the field by the local church on the banks of the River Severn in 1910, after being evicted from their old Copthorne Barracks home.

A Main Stand was built on the east side of the ground in 1922 and was extended towards the north side in 1938, where a year previously work had just been completed on what was known as the Station End, which was built over a five-year period. The opposite terrace behind the south goal was known as the Wakeman End, after the School – whose windows overlook the pitch – was built behind it. The Main Stand was covered in its entirety in 1966 when work was completed towards the Wakeman End of the ground, giving it a capacity of 18,000.

But there was a price to pay for its idyllic setting: the burst banks of the River Severn frequently swamped Gay Meadow, particularly during the mid-20th century. The construction of dams attempted to alleviate the problem, and were largely successful.

Despite the postcard location, however, the reality of poor access, potential flooding and no room for expansion meant that Town had no choice but to move on, and, with a reduced capacity of 8,000 after the Taylor Report, they left for their 9,800-seater New Meadow home in 2007; it is currently named the Prostar Stadium for sponsorship reasons.

Demolition of the old stadium began in September 2007, and by October the ground was reduced to rubble. The site has been earmarked for residential building, but the depressed economic climate had, at the time of writing, caused plans to stall.

MEMORIES

As a resident of Nottingham, I am one of the so-called exiles supporting Shrewsbury Town. Where I am unusual is that I was an exile before I'd even heard of the club. I was born in Oldham to a Latics-supporting father, so the odds of me ever stepping through the turnstiles at the Gay Meadow were not high; Boundary Park must have looked my more logical home.

However, I had a Shropshire-born mother, and by the time I was about eight years old we were living in north Shropshire. It is not surprising therefore that my first match was Shrewsbury versus Oldham in October 1965, and I started cheering for Salop for no other reason than to annoy my Dad, and I have been cheering for them ever since. It was also a

good start to my life as a fan, with Shrewsbury beating Oldham 3–1 on that day.

In the early days I used to watch with my Dad from the enclosure, a standing area along the side nearest the Wakeman End, which has been all seating now for some time. However, when Dad decided I was old enough to go to matches on my own, I hung out with school friends at the Station End, joining in the singing.

I also remember when some supporters moved to the halfway line along the Riverside, and after a couple of games of them making more noise than the Station End, the group I was with decided to join them. Before long, the Riverside became the main focus for singing Town fans and, not long after, the club made it official by turning the Station End into the away end.

My favourite player in those days was Alf Wood, first as a centre-half and then as a goal-scoring forward. He sometimes wasn't the most delicate of players, and I still smile when I recall him bounding towards the touchline to intercept an opponent. Said opponent though was no mug, and at the sight of Alf bearing down on him cleverly sidestepped at the last second.

Poor Alf couldn't stop himself and collided first with the linesman and then a policeman before careering off down the tunnel. The sheepish look on his face was priceless as he reappeared between the prone figures of the linesman and policeman and was greeted with a cheer from the crowd.

At another game, he managed a bigger cheer, as well as assorted wolf whistles, when an enthusiastic opponent managed to rip off his shorts during a tackle. Looking rather embarrassed, he stood there for what seemed like ages in his underwear while the kit man dashed back to the dressing room to fetch a spare pair.

There are many more memories of the old ground over the years and it was heartbreaking when we moved to the soulless new ground that we are in now. The Gay Meadow was our home and we should have stayed there.

Steve Rogerson

THE DELL – SOUTHAMPTON

Name:
The Dell

Highest attendance:
31,044, vs. Manchester United,
8 October 1969

First league match:
Southampton 4–0 Swindon Town,
30 August 1920

Final league match:
Southampton 3–2 Arsenal,
19 May 2001

Memorable moment:
Southampton 4–0 West Bromwich Albion,
17 February 1976
(FA Cup fifth round replay)

Current stadium:
St Mary's Stadium

Battling through several wartime attacks and surviving to stage Southampton's greatest games, the Dell finally succumbed to the desire for a newer stadium after 103 years, and the houses in its place now honour the club's own heroic veterans.

The Saints moved from the County Cricket Ground in 1898 after their rapid success and swelling crowds meant they needed a new home. The Dell was built on the site of a pond, which had to be converted into several streams that were forced underground for the stadium to be built on top. The ground initially had stands on the east and west sides flanking the pitch, with a capacity of 24,000.

Both stands would not last long, however, as the west was replaced in 1925 with a double-deck structure that largely survived until the Dell's final day, while the east was ravaged by fire four years later, a slightly smaller mirror-image double-decker rapidly emerging in its place.

The Dell's proximity to Southampton docks meant the stadium was always at risk of attack during World War II, and in November 1940 a bomb struck the ground towards the Milton Road End, caused a giant crater that exposed one of the underground streams, causing major flooding. An armaments explosion in the West Stand also caused damage, though the resulting fire was rapidly doused. Southampton played the majority of their wartime games away from home.

To accommodate a post-war boom in attendances, the club created two-tiered uncovered terracing on the Milton Road End by building platforms on top of the existing banking. These became known as the 'chocolate boxes', but lasted only until the 1980s when they were taken down. The end terraces at the stadium were distinctive, as roads running behind them caused the ground to look like a parallelogram owing to their slanting nature.

In the wake of the Hillsborough disaster the Dell became an all-seater stadium, but this reduced its capacity to just 15,000 – the smallest in the top division at the time. With Southampton annually scraping survival in the Premier League, the decision was made to move away in 1998 to the £32 million St Mary's Stadium in 2001.

The Dell was converted to housing, with the apartment blocks named after former club legends like Matt Le Tissier and Mick Channon. The club's subsequent fall from grace in both League standing and financial stability has perhaps proved the grass is not always greener.

MEMORIES

A relative fortress compared to St Mary's; Saints rarely suffered defeat, probably because the fans were so close to the pitch that it inhibited the visiting team's performance.

Memories of the terraces where, if you were vertically challenged, then you would be constantly moving from side to side trying to see (like plant stems moving in the wind); if you were the opposite, then you ran the risk of abuse from the large Stevedore contingent of those times for blocking their view!

More recent memories, when seating areas became mandatory, of the 'low-spec' wooden benches, when you came out at the end of the game with a back covered in bruises from

the constant attack by knobbly knees; although this would largely go unnoticed when Saints were playing well and winning! Particular memories include Mick Channon against Fulham: when his route to goal was blocked by the goalkeeper and defender, he stopped the ball, looked up, waited, and then drilled the ball past the amazed players!

Going to an FA Cup game against Nottingham Forest without tickets, getting in for the last 15 minutes and seeing Saints score the winner from a young, inexperienced and small striker called Steve Moran who defied logic for a few seasons to score numerous goals against the best defences in the land!

Perhaps the best memories are those relating to the more

experienced players who came to the Dell in their later years, 'past it' as the press would state (such as Peter Osgood, Frank Worthington, Charlie George), who gave the fans a master class of deft touches, intelligent positioning and energy saving movement!

Neil Barron

HAIG AVENUE – SOUTHPORT

Name:

Haig Avenue

Highest attendance:

20,111, vs. Newcastle United,
26 January 1932

First league match:

Southport 1–1 Durham City,
27 August 1921

Final league match:

Southport 1–1 Huddersfield,
22 April 1978

Memorable moment:

Southport 1–0 Bradford Park Avenue,
14 February 1931 (FA Cup fifth round)

Current stadium:

Haig Avenue

Alongside Anfield, Goodison Park and Prenton Park, Southport FC's Haig Avenue stadium completed a quartet of Football League grounds in Merseyside for a large part of the 20th century before they lost their League status in 1978. Opened in 1905, it was originally christened Ash Lane before being named in honour of Earl Haig coinciding with Southport's election to the Football League in 1921.

A wooden grandstand pre-dated Southport's election to the League, having been relocated from their former home on Scarisbrick New Road, but the new era was celebrated by a covered terrace erected opposite, running the full length of the pitch. In 1932 it was extended around the east side of the ground to the Scarisbrick New Road End.

An all-too-common culprit – a carelessly discarded cigarette butt – was suspected to have caused Haig Avenue's original wooden grandstand to perish in flames in 1966. Replaced two years later, the stand still survives today. 1978 saw Southport drop out of the League, losing a re-election vote to Wigan Athletic.

In the wake of the Valley Parade fire, the covered terracing running from the popular side to behind the west goal was demolished, leaving the ground a sorry sight. Southport's ambition to eventually rejoin the League saw the club build new uncovered terracing around the Popular Side and Blowick Road End, and a new covered terrace behind the Scarisbrick Road End, renaming it the Jack Carr Stand after a deceased former president.

While never quite reaching the heights of their Merseyside neighbours, Southport enjoyed an eventful League existence, fluctuating between the Third and Fourth Divisions, perhaps the highlight being the club's FA Cup run of 1930–31, where Haig Avenue witnessed a fifth round victory over Bradford Park Avenue that set up a Merseyside derby quarter-final against Everton. With Southport only two promotions away from a return to the League, Merseyside could yet regain its quartet of football stadiums.

MEMORIES

From Friday-night crowds of 5,000 and an eighth-place finish in the old Division Three (League One now), to the modern-day following of under a thousand in Blue Square North, the aspirations of following one's hometown club have changed markedly over the past 43 years.

Southport's decline from their peak in the 1960s to Football League demotion in the '70s meant rare fulfilment of fans' dreams – apart from, of course, the momentous Fourth Division Championship triumph in 1973.

Friday night football at Haig Avenue was something to look forward to after a week of school for this teenager! Memories of the Blowick and 'Brick ends during the rare good times are still fresh and clear, but since the League days, interest within the town has been apathetic at best.

The Yellows' main non-League achievement was the 1998 FA Trophy final, with a decent local following travelling to Wembley to witness a brave but narrow defeat.

A couple of promotions within the non-League structure should have kick-started Southport's push for a return to former glories, but under current conditions such a dream seems highly unlikely.

I do, however, together with Sandgrounders worldwide, hope that one day we can all 'live the dream' once again.

Phil Marrow

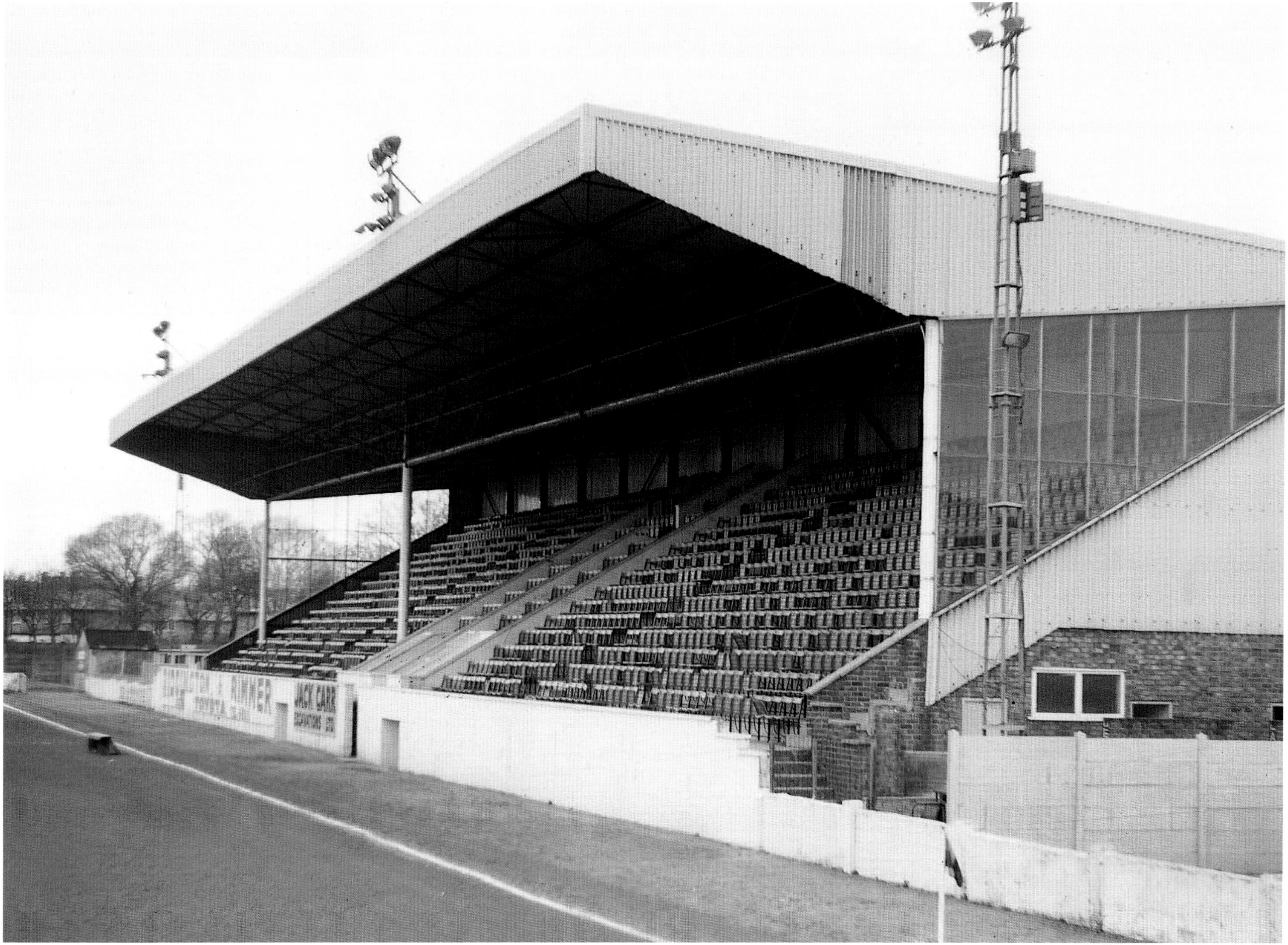
RIMMER
TOYOTA
JACK CARR
EXCAVATIONS LTD

MUIRTON PARK – ST JOHNSTONE

Name:
Muirton Park

Highest attendance:
29,972, vs. Dundee,
10 February 1951

First league match:
St Johnstone 1–0 Queen's Park,
25 December 1924

Final league match:
St Johnstone 0–1 Ayr United,
29 April 1989

Memorable moment:
St Johnstone 3–0 Hamburg,
29 September 1971
(UEFA Cup first round)

Current stadium:
McDiarmid Park

Scottish Premier League side St Johnstone called Muirton Park home after they left the recreation area of a nearby prison in 1924. The club from Perth decided the recreation grounds were too costly to develop further after a near four-decade residence and set up camp at the new stadium, all open terracing save for a concrete and steel grandstand on the west side of the ground.

It would be nearly another 40 years before any modifications were carried out to the stadium, with a covered enclosure constructed opposite the Main Stand. The club endured a roller-coaster existence at Muirton, yo-yoing between the country's top two divisions. The Muirton Park trophy cabinet played host to four League Championships, the first being the old Division Two title in the Saints' debut season at the ground. European football arrived in 1971 after a third-place finish in the top flight, the highlight of the adventure being a demolition of German giants Hamburg in September.

As the 1980s approached the club found itself in financial difficulties, and after the Bradford fire at Valley Parade it quickly became clear the ground would become another victim of the Safety At Sports Grounds Act, with their grandstand's wooden flooring and seating having not been replaced since the its original erection.

The club received a lucrative offer from supermarket giant Asda whereby the chain would pay for a new purpose-built stadium to be built elsewhere in return for the old site. The club accepted and moved to McDiarmid Park in 1989, named after the farmer who donated the land.

MEMORIES

One very personal memory to me: I was fortunate enough to be the last mascot at the old ground in April 1989. Not a very lucky one, however, as we lost the game 1–0 to Ayr United! A crowd of over 7,000 saw the game and being in the dressing room prior to kick-off the atmosphere was tremendous. The players were in party mode and I recall the late Gary Thomson starting a 'Bonnie Wee Jeannie McColl' singalong as I sat on the treatment table! Meeting all the players who played that day was great and leading the team out was immense!

My only regret was that I never got a commemorative badge as only folk who paid at the turnstiles got one!
Ryan Murray

LOVE STREET – ST MIRREN

Name:
Love Street
Highest attendance:
47,438, vs. Celtic,
20 August 1949
First league match:
St Mirren 0–3 Celtic,
8 September 1894
Final league match:
St Mirren 0–0 Motherwell,
3 January 2009
Memorable moment:
St Mirren 1–0 Tromsø,
16 September 1987
(European Cup Winners' Cup first round)
Current stadium:
New St Mirren Park

When many of a certain age hear the title 'Love Street' they may think of the 1968 track by American rock band the Doors – but the romantically titled stadium was actually St Mirren's fifth home when they arrived in 1894, despite being in existence less than two decades. They moved from nearby Thistle Park.

With an original capacity of just 1,000, much of St Mirren's early tenure at Love Street was spent securing the rights to the narrow plot of land from the owner, who nearly forced them out after a decade by drastically increasing the rent.

Upon securing ownership of the site in 1921, St Mirren went about implementing grand plans for a 60,000-capacity terraced arena, its crown jewel a grandstand seating nearly 5,000. The Great Depression put paid to this idea. There was minimal redeveloping – save the North Bank becoming covered in the 1950s – until 1979 when the Love Street End was demolished and rebuilt, but seating was not installed for nearly another 30 years.

Luck would dictate that St Mirren's 1987 Scottish Cup success was played almost exclusively away from Love Street, but it did bring European football to the ground the following season, in which the Saints recorded a 1–0 success over Norwegian side Tromsø. 1995 saw the large West Stand built but the benefactor who aided its construction soon fell into financial trouble and began an uncertain time in the history of the club.

The act of securing their home nearly 90 years earlier paid off in 2007 when the club was suffering from crippling debts and its future was in doubt. The decision was made to sell the stadium to supermarket giant Tesco for enough money to fend off the debt collectors and build a new stadium a mile away that reached SPL standards, leaving thousands of St Mirren fans mourning their one true love.

MEMORIES

It was late 1968, Scottish football was on a high and Colin Stein had just joined Rangers for the first Scottish six-figure transfer fee. His first two outings ended with hat-tricks against Arbroath and Hibs; next up was St Mirren at a foggy Love Street. Our star winger was Hugh Gilshan, who joined from local junior side Johnstone Burgh; his fee was a set of training tops and the promise of a pre-season friendly.

Stein was anonymous apart from a booking, and Gilshan appeared out of the mist late in the game to give us a 1–0 victory in front of 35,000 fans!
billyg

ANNFIELD STADIUM – STIRLING ALBION

Name:
Annfield Stadium
Highest attendance:
38,600, vs. Celtic,
14 March 1959
First league match:
Stirling Albion 4–1 Ayr United,
27 August 1947
Final league match:
Stirling Albion 2–0 Clydebank,
2 May 1992
Memorable moment:
Stirling Albion 1–1 Queen's Park,
30 April 1977
(Stirling Albion lift the Scottish Second Division title)
Current stadium:
Forthbank Stadium

Not to be confused with the spiritual home of the Merseyside giants, Annfield Stadium was the base of Scottish minnows Stirling Albion who spent 48 years there following their inception in 1945. A mere three-month period preceded Albion's first match, so as a consequence the ground was very basic, just uncovered embankment around the pitch.

Monetary troubles were never far from the club and in 1981 it made the decision to sell the stadium to the local council and rent it back to ease debts. But little work had been done in previous years and the ground was in a dilapidated state.

While Annfield's existence was short, it dabbled in innovation, becoming the first stadium in Scotland to employ an artificial pitch in 1987 when it was decided it was too costly to maintain a grass playing surface. The new surface coincided with the renovation of the terracing and crush barriers, making Annfield the best it had looked in years. The experiment did not last long, however, as many complained about the surface, and it ultimately led Albion out of Annfield.

The decision was made to leave as the cost of upgrading the stadium and reverting back to grass turf was deemed more expensive than a complete relocation. As the club no longer owned the stadium, it was sold off to create housing in 1992. Stirling Albion would have to wait 11 months before moving into their new home, meanwhile playing their games at Stenhousemuir's Ochilview Park. While sharing a name with the iconic stadium south of the border, Stirling's Annfield lacked the glitz and glamour, but made up for it in rugged footballing charm.

MEMORIES

At four years old, I started to be a ball boy, mostly at reserve matches to start with and then onto first team matches. One of the ball boy memories I have was trying to cover the whole four sides of the pitch myself at a very early age during a reserve match.

For the next 10 years I was a ball boy up until I was 14 at the end of the 1989/90 season. During those times I was often picked upon by the other ball boys – I don't know whether it was because my dad was now in charge of the ball boys or was it because I was just a spoiled little brat? Probably the latter!

During my school years I would go up to Annfield during the school holidays, while my mum worked (or played the fruit machine all day). Those were classic times; my mum worked with the late Bruce McDonald the groundsman and he would allow me to go onto the Annfield turf myself and I would have a game of football in my full Albion kit and boots.

Whether it was playing pool for free in the members' bar, being scared out my wits to go anywhere near the Annfield Mansion House, driving the grass mower and then playing on the Astroturf after reserve matches with other supporters, it was all one happy memory.

Around about the age of 13 to 15, I would also look after the Albion dressing rooms alongside my dad at Annfield and during those years I also sold match programmes and on one occasion was assigned to a turnstile for a match.

I could go on and on and go over so many more happy memories, especially from Annfield Park and famous Albion matches I have witnessed.

Scott McLean

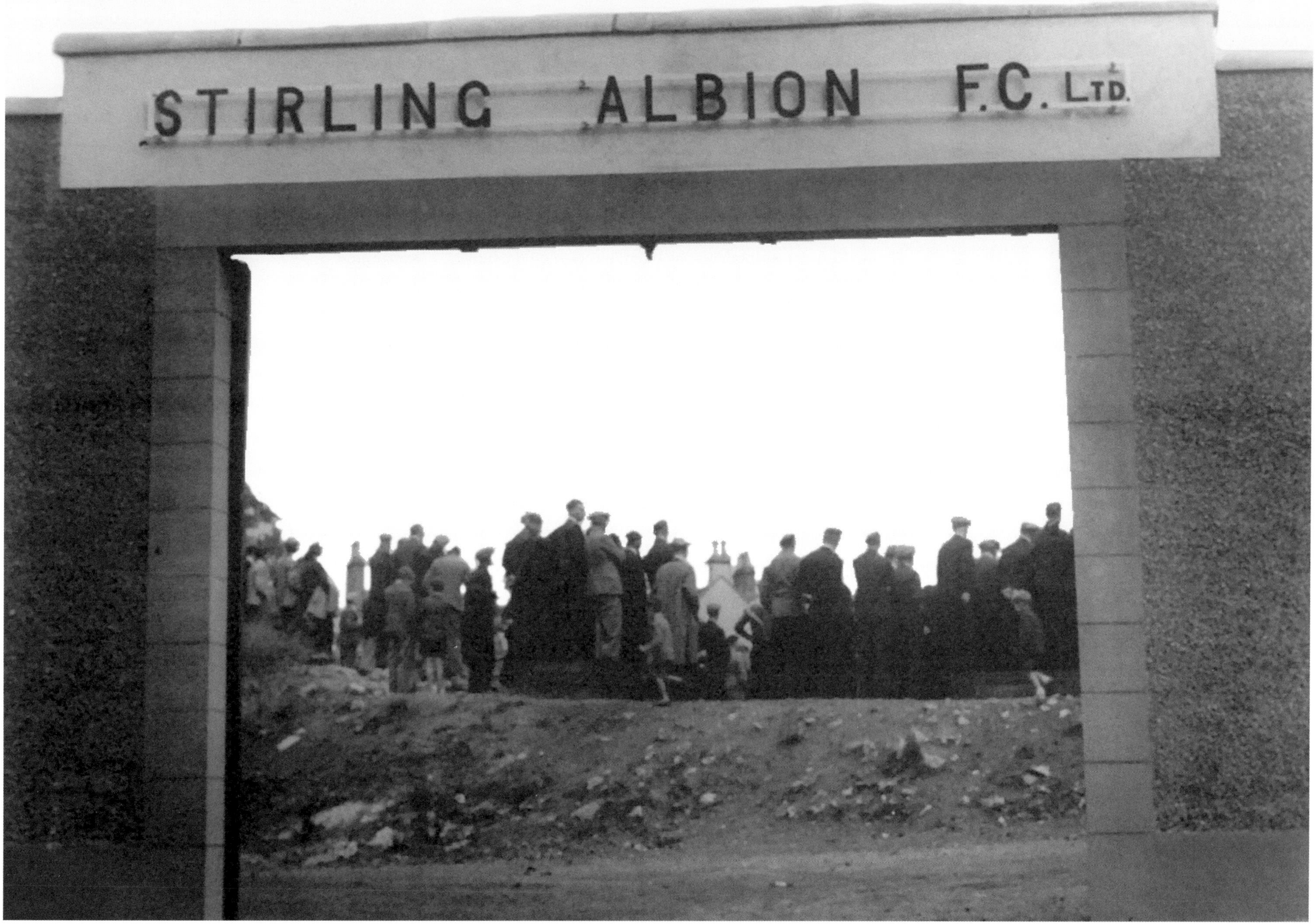
STIRLING ALBION F.C. LTD.

VICTORIA GROUND – STOKE CITY

Name:
Victoria Ground
Highest attendance:
51,380, vs. Arsenal,
29 March 1937
First league match:
Stoke City 0–2 West Bromwich Albion,
8 September 1888
Final league match:
Stoke City 2–1 West Bromwich Albion,
4 May 1997
Memorable moment:
Stoke City 2–0 Luton Town,
18 May 1963
(Stoke win Second Division title)
Current stadium:
Britannia Stadium

Stoke City stayed at their Victoria Ground stadium for 119 years – an English record only now set to be surpassed by Wolverhampton Wanderers' stay at Molineux. City themselves are also considered the country's second oldest League football team after Notts County – both the club and its home are integral parts of the British game.

The club switched to the site from the adjacent Sweetings Fields in 1878 as Stoke FC, having changed their name from Stoke Ramblers. It was originally a large oval expanse of banking, with just one small stand on the east side. Stoke's early years saw them drop in and out of the League, but when they returned for the second time in 1919 they had another small stand, this time on the Butler Street side.

The decade-long period between 1925 and '35 was busy for the club; it was renamed Stoke City FC in light of the amalgamation of the towns of the Potteries and five years later the Boothen End was covered and terraced. A further five years saw the Butler Street Stand rebuilt with an impressive barrel roof and a seating capacity of 5,000.

The Main Stand was modernised in 1963, and nearly a decade later in 1972, after City qualified for Europe, the Butler Street Stand roof was blown off by a gale. As the 1980s approached work was completed on a two-tiered Stoke End behind the goal, seating 4,000 spectators.

Despite the recommendations of the Taylor Report in the 1990s, the Victoria Ground looked well-equipped to adapt. It looked as if Stoke City would stay for many more years to come, but in 1996 the decision was made by chief executive Jez Moxey to move to a state-of-the-art 28,000-seater stadium. The site of the Victoria Ground unusually still remains undeveloped, a fitting tribute perhaps to one of the country's oldest football sites.

MEMORIES

The Boothen End was a mass of swaying bodies and was rammed every week even though the crowd was 7,000 if you listen to folk talk about it! My memory of the Vic was its location and the steam coming from the showers on a winter's day bellowing out over the Boothen Paddock and up into the Boothen Stand. Ah, the memories.
Werrington

At a night match you could see clouds and clouds of cigarette smoke in the light of the floodlights disappearing into the sky, and someone selling hamburgers by the corner of the Stoke End.

The Vic, the Cabin and supporters' club for a beer. Hiding in Stoke churchyard for the away fans, being bitten by a police dog in the very same place. Beating Arsenal and Leeds, watching Mancs burn their scarves on the Stoke End when they were relegated.

Playing Ajax, watching Hudson, Greenhoff and co. The crush to get in the ground 10 minutes before kick off. Happy days, apart from getting beat!
Eddieclamp

ROKER PARK – SUNDERLAND

Name:
Roker Park

Highest attendance:
75,118, vs. Derby County,
8 March 1933

First league match:
Sunderland 1–0 Liverpool,
10 September 1898

Final league match:
Sunderland 3–0 Everton,
3 May 1997

Memorable moment:
Italy 2–0 Chile, 13 July 1966
(World Cup group match)

Current stadium:
Stadium of Light

Sunderland's stay at Roker Park ended in 1997, just one year shy of a century. Yet its trophy cabinet was always well stocked, Sunderland obtaining no less than 10 pieces of silverware while at their home. The stadium had three basic stands when Sunderland moved in, but in 1912 the Roker End was enlarged using an intricate arrangement of concrete beams to support it, a unique feature that would last for 70 years.

Archibald Leitch was brought in to design Roker Park's new Grandstand, which opened in 1929, giving the stadium a capacity of 60,000. Seven years later the Leitch-designed Clock Stand was constructed, housing an impressive 15,500. Bombing in World War II did little to halt the continued work on Roker Park and in 1966 it was selected as a World Cup venue ahead of St James Park. Temporary seating was installed and the Fulwell End was covered in anticipation.

The part-demolition of the Roker End in 1982 was the beginning of the end for the stadium. The Taylor Report in 1989 dictated that it needed to become all-seater, but meeting this requirement would decrease its capacity severely, a constraint unacceptable for a club competing in the top division.

The decision was made to relocate, but it wasn't until 1997 that Sunderland vacated Roker Park for good, moving to the 42,000 Stadium of Light, leaving their old home for housing development. The lavishly titled stadium, while state of the art, lacks for now the rugged, asymmetrical feel of the Mackems' old home.

MEMORIES

It was our home, I didn't want to leave and it's still my spiritual home.

I watched about 450 matches there over 20 years, some great times, and it was a different era. I left at the end of the Liverpool match slightly earlier than my mates as I had to go to night shift and I looked back one last time with a tear in my eye.

When I first entered the Stadium of Light for the Ajax match I stood at the top of the ramp and just looked in awe and the size of the ground, the glinting of the lush, damp pitch and the sheer size of the place. In a moment I realised I was wrong to want to stay at Roker. I feel a little guilty about that. The previous chairmen, Cowie and Murray, had allowed Roker to decay beyond saving and we had no choice but to move on.

However, we should have kept more of our roots. Our old badge perhaps? At the very least named the East Stand the Roker Avenue Stand or named the Stadium New Roker or Monkwearmouth. We tried to sweep our history away when it was all that the club had for many years.
Keith S30S

Like lots of fans, I remember trying out different parts of the ground. First games were in the Roker End - I can still hear a man nearby shouting 'He'll do for us!' during the first half of George Mulhall's home debut in 1962 (3–1 v Luton). Then it was the Fulwell, or were our season tickets in the Main Stand Paddock before that? Clock Stand Paddock came much later, after I'd moved down south, but I definitely stood there on occasions (including the famous Man United cup replay when we were somehow just swept in after the ground was supposed to be full).
Colin

VETCH FIELD – SWANSEA CITY

Name:
Vetch Field

Highest attendance:
32,796, vs. Arsenal,
17 February 1968

First league match:
Swansea City 2–1 Watford, 2 September 1920

Final league match:
Swansea City 1–0 Shrewsbury,
30 April 2005

Memorable moment:
Swansea City 2–0 Liverpool,
16 February 1982
(memorable result beating the eventual
League champions)

Current stadium:
Liberty Stadium

Named after the plant that grew on the site, Vetch Field became the home of Swansea Town from 1912, having previously played host to amateur outfit Swansea Villa. The first stand was erected at the beginning of the club's tenancy before the stadium even had turf.

The first incarnation of the West Stand behind the goal was built in 1927. It would be another three decades before more stands would join it, supporters paying for the North Bank terracing to be covered before floodlights were installed a year later in 1960.

This preceded Swansea – renamed City in 1970 – plummeting from the old Second Division towards the Football League trapdoor, finishing bottom of the 92 in 1975 but gaining a reprieve through re-election. Happier times at the Vetch Field followed as they rocketed from the basement tier to the top of the entire League in just over three years under former Welsh international John Toshack.

A new two-tiered East Stand was completed in 1981. There were further plans for it to wrap around and replace the dilapidated Main Stand, largely unaltered since its construction in 1912, but the money never materialised to complete it. The 1990s saw the second tier of the West Stand built over amid safety concerns in the wake of the Hillsborough and Valley Parade disasters.

This was an early indicator that the Vetch Field may no longer have been suited to Swansea City, and sure enough, in 2005 the club left their home to take up residence in a new purpose-built arena shared with the Ospreys Rugby Union club. The new home replaced an old athletics stadium on the same site. The Vetch Field remained untouched for years after the club's departure, though unfortunately its indigenous plant did not return!

MEMORIES

Samson had his hair, Swansea have the North Bank. Well, had the North Bank.

The source of Swansea's strength waved goodbye to their home yesterday as the curtain finally fell on league football at Vetch Field, 85 years after it first arrived. And although the game itself hardly did justice to the occasion, it didn't seem to matter all that much to the 11,469 crammed into the ground like sardines.

A few more clambered up ladders to have a sneaky peak over the wall or from surrounding rooftops. Thankfully, no prisoners from the local jailhouse made it on to theirs. I know, because I was there.

But had they done so, no doubt they would have found it hard not to be swept up in the party atmosphere. The raw emotion that spilled forth when the final whistle sounded put the day up there with any of the heart-stopping moments the Vetch has witnessed in its 93-year history.

There will be dissenting voices of course. 'What about the day in 2003 when we beat Hull to stay in the Football League or the time mighty Leeds were thrashed 5–1, 24 years ago on our First Division debut?' they will say.

The debate will rightly rage for years over which was the more memorable.

But there was so much about yesterday that tugged on the heartstrings of not just Swansea fans but also anyone else who was in the vicinity.

April 30, 2005, will live long in the memory of Swans fans. Something that there can be no denying is that the dilapidated ground which became so familiar to fans that it was known affectionately by its first name has seen it all since the gates first opened for a Southern League game with Cardiff in September 1912 - the highs, the lows and plenty of in-betweens.

Now, just like the Dell, Roker Park and countless other famous Football League fortresses of yesteryear, it has come time to say goodbye!

Wales On Sunday, May 2005

CATKIN PARK – THIRD LANARK

Name:
Cathkin Park

Highest attendance:
45,455, vs. Glasgow Rangers,
27 February 1954

First league match:
Third Lanark 2–1 Heart of Midlothian,
22 August 1903

Final league match:
Third Lanark 3–3 Queen of the South,
25 April 1967

Memorable moment:
Third Lanark 2–1 Hibernian, 30 April 1904
(Third Lanark lift the Scottish League title)

Current stadium:
N/A

Cathkin Park played host to the only club to win the Scottish League only to go out of business years later. Third Lanark topped the Scottish game in 1904, winning their only Scottish League title. Various Cup final appearances and successes also peppered the team's history, not what one would expect from a club that would cease to exist 60 years later.

Cathkin Park was originally named Hampden Park when it was home to Queens Park from 1884, but the club took the name with them when they moved a few yards to Scotland's national stadium in 1903, where they remain to this day.

Third Lanark's new stadium was home to many of the Glaswegians who enjoyed football but did not want to be associated with the sectarian complications that came with the Old Firm of Celtic and Rangers. Third Lanark immediately took to their new home, winning the Scottish League in their first season there.

A 100-goal high preceded the ultimate of lows for both the club and the stadium; Third Lanark finished third in the Scottish League in 1961, scoring a century of goals in the process, but relegation followed just four years later. The club was declared bankrupt in 1967 amid accusations of financial mismanagement that persist to this day.

Large areas of the vast oval terracing still remain at Cathkin Park, though covered in parts with masses of green trees, and the reformed Third Lanark amateur team occasionally plays there. The stadium serves as a poignant reminder that no League club is safe from financial perils in the modern game.

MEMORIES

The ground itself seems to have a magical aura. It is a far cry from awe-inspiring modern arenas, but its soul is palpable. Perhaps the tears and nostalgia of generations have provided nourishment, but the playing surface is in fine condition, and the terracing does not seem empty, though no one is in sight. It is a Ground guaranteed to stimulate the hairs on the back of the neck.

'There is definitely an eerie presence to the ground,' observed the notable Scottish football writer, Bob Crampsey, who remembers the club fondly, and whose house overlooks Cathkin Park.
***Scotland On Sunday*, July 1999**

There is no stopping the human tide at a Cathkin Park cup-tie against Rangers in 1961. Official attendance was 37,000. Rumours of boardroom skulduggery were rife as Thirds folded despite healthy gates and bumper transfer windfalls.

Cathkin and Hampden are just a stone's throw apart...but Third's derelict ground is now a haven for dog-walkers.
***Glasgow Evening Times*, June 2007**

FELLOWS PARK – WALSALL

Name:

Fellows Park

Highest attendance:

25,453, vs. Newcastle United,
29 August 1961

First league match:

Walsall 2–0 Burton Wanderers,
5 September 1896

Final league match:

Walsall 1–1 Rotherham United,
1 May 1990

Memorable moment:

Walsall 2–0 Arsenal, 14 January 1933
(FA Cup third round)

Current stadium:

Bescot Stadium

Walsall moved to Fellows Park in 1896, when it was originally known by its location as Hillary Street. Within four years the club found itself playing back at its former home on West Bromwich Road after rent difficulties before returning to Hillary Street for a barren 20-year period of non-League football. In 1930, nine years after the club's return to the League, the ground was renamed Fellows Park in honour of the chairman who supported them during their years in the football doldrums.

The early 1930s saw the Main Stand constructed, though it only ran along part of the length of the pitch. This was extended in 1975 to accommodate over 1,000 more seated spectators, as well as partially covering the front paddock. The stadium consisted of only three sides until 1960 when the north side of the ground, occupied by laundry buildings, became a small terrace. The Hillary Street End terrace opposite was covered five years later.

The ground was not known for its aesthetic qualities; the Hillary Street End roof was staggered in size, and the Main Stand built in different stages gave it a thrown-together look. When it suffered through safety restrictions and had its capacity halved in 1985, thoughts began to turn towards a new stadium.

The last three seasons at Fellows Park were certainly eventful; a promotion to Division Two was quickly followed by two bottom-placed finishes, ensuring Walsall bid farewell to their home in far from happy circumstances. From 1990 they faced their future in the League's basement division – and though they've dragged themselves up a level on a number of occasions since, the club would hope their new home would not endure another two decades in the footballing wilderness.

MEMORIES

Several things spring to mind about Fellows Park. First, that it had atmosphere with 3,000 in the ground – I imagine because being terracing, we all crowded together for warmth and safety.

There always tended to be mass movements of people around the terraces since the home terraces stretched without interruption from the home end right around one side of the ground under the Cowsheds, opposite the Main Stand. So if we were playing towards the goal at the far end, especially in the second half, most of the noisiest part of the home end crowd would move around the side of the ground to the far end of the Cowshed Terrace.

In latter years this placed us close to the fences and the 'dead zone' between us and the away fans, who of course because they wanted to get as near as possible to the goal their team were playing towards, and because we were so young and handsome and therefore attractive to be close to, were then just on the other side of the fence; the gap in between was patrolled by two or three nervous-looking police with dogs.

Since contrary to misty-eyed memory the football was not always so riveting that we were glued to it, we had to find ways to entertain ourselves. Being vile to the opposition fans was not cricket, so we barked at the dogs instead – and you can imagine the effect of 2,000 football fans barking at three dogs. And the more mental they went, the more we barked, since it was increasingly funny to see their handlers trying to keep the dogs from launching themselves at the fence, towards the barking humans who already smelled enticingly of warm meat pies and Bovril.

Probably our greatest hour: clutching victory from the jaws of ignominy. In the 1988 play-off final, back in the days when this was played home and away over two legs, we had beaten Bristol City 3–1 at their place, but then again has not turned up for the home leg and lost 2–0 to a team led by fearsome player manager Joe Jordan. We contrived to win the penalty shoot-out, which gave us home advantage for the replay. Fellows Park was heaving, and absolutely buzzing, and the fans, like the players, were finally up for it.

The noise was immense, and simply rose in volume, as we roared into a 3–0 lead in the first quarter of the match. David Kelly's hat-trick goal in the second half (this one at least in front of the home faithful) secured a 4–0 victory, and a place in Division Two (when it was the real, full-fat Division Two, I'll have you know!). Of course, Kelly was sold to West Ham in the close season, never replaced, and down we fell two divisions in the next two seasons, to start our new life in a new stadium in the League basement. But just for a moment, we were actually quite good.

fensaddler

WEMBLEY STADIUM

Name:

Wembley Stadium

Highest attendance:

126,047,

Bolton Wanderers 2–0 West Ham United,

28 April 1923

Memorable moment:

England 4–2 West Germany,

30 July 1966

Current stadium:

Wembley Stadium

Despite being known as the Home of Football, Wembley Stadium was only completed as recently as 1923, when clubs like Stoke City had already been at their stadium for 35 years. But Wembley instantly found itself at the heart of the country's sporting landscape.

Originally built for the British Empire Exhibition – showcasing the best of King George V's vast empire – interest peaked when the FA signed up for Cup finals to be played at the new stadium. So high was the expectation that the attendance at its first match, the famed 'White Horse Final', remained the record for the duration of its existence. The record shows the venue to have been full to capacity, though reports suggest there could have been anywhere up to double that amount for the game.

Floodlights were installed in 1955, much later than with most clubs, and it was the beginning of Wembley's updating. The stadium was originally uncovered at both goal ends, until major renovation in 1963 saw the whole structure covered in state-of-the-art roofing. Three years later saw the venue's finest hour: England capturing the World Cup on home soil in a final that is part of the fabric of the country.

Aside from cup finals, Wembley held the final of the League divisional competition play-off system after its inauguration in the 1986–87 season. The first play-off finals did not occur at Wembley until 1990, when all was decided on a single game rather than over two legs.

Though football was the undoubted jewel in the Wembley crown, the stadium's main revenue was from greyhound racing, speedway, rock concerts and other sporting events; the annual competition finals were not enough to keep the giant venue open.

In 1999 the FA announced that the old Wembley with its iconic twin towers, symbolic of the British Empire, would be coming down and in its place would be built a brand new 90,000-seater stadium, to open in 2003. It would be four years after this predicted date that the new stadium actually opened; the Millennium Stadium in Cardiff had taken on its obligations in the meantime.

The curtain came down on the Home of Football with another twist in the rivalry between England and old enemies Germany. The latter gained some measure of revenge for the 1966 World Cup final by defeating England 0–1 in a 2002 World Cup qualifier, ensuring the country bade a sobering goodbye to its most famous stadium.

The graceful arc of the current Wembley is some consolation for the lack of the old Twin Towers, and the stadium became the centrepiece of a bid for the 2018 World Cup.

MEMORIES

The White Horse Final: April 28, 1923. Probably the most dramatic FA Cup final ever. Official attendance figures were 126,047 but a crowd of at least 220,000 crammed into the stadium – more than twice the number for any other cup final.

Fans spilled on to the pitch until PC George Albert Scorey, mounted on a magnificent white horse called Billy, showed up to disperse the throng. He recalled: 'I could see nothing but a sea of heads. But I told myself not to be beaten.' The game started 40 minutes late and Bolton won 2–0.

England v Germany, 1966, our finest hour as a footballing nation. More than 93,000 fans watched England beat Germany 4–2 in extra time.

Geoff Hurst's amazing drive into the net in the dying seconds was encapsulated forever by BBC commentator Kenneth Wolstenholme who said: 'Some people are on the pitch – they think it's all over. It is now.' Sir Geoff says: 'The noise from the crowd was at such a crescendo, it made the hairs stand up on the back of my neck. The thought of it still does. When it's reduced to rubble, the stadium will still hold many memories for me.'

England team-mate Nobby Stiles said: 'Playing at Wembley has always been a special day out. The atmosphere hits you as soon as you walk out of the tunnel.'

The Mirror, October 2000

SPRINGFIELD PARK – WIGAN ATHLETIC

Name:
Springfield Park

Highest attendance:
30,443, vs. Sheffield Wednesday,
19 January 1929

First league match:
Wigan Athletic 0–3 Grimsby Town,
23 August 1978

Final league match:
Wigan Athletic 1–1 Manchester City,
15 May 1999

Memorable moment:
Wigan 2–0 Mansfield Town,
3 May 1997
(Wigan win Third Division title)

Current stadium:
DW Stadium

Springfield Park is best known for housing Wigan Athletic from their formation until 1999. It hosted League football from 1978, but the first time the stadium tasted League action was some 46 years earlier when Wigan Borough briefly graced the Third Division North from its inception in 1921 until 1932.

The ground was built and opened in 1897 and in total played host to five separate clubs bearing the Wigan name, but Athletic were undoubtedly the most successful. They began their tenure in the wake of Borough's demise in 1932.

The stadium consisted of the Town and Shelvington Ends behind the goals, the latter with a rather unusual grassy verge at the top of its banking, the Popular Side terracing, and the large Main Stand that sat in the middle of the length of my pitch. The original had been levelled by fire in 1953, its replacement one of the best in non-League football.

Only one trophy was lifted at Springfield Park in its entire history, secured when Athletic beat Mansfield Town 2–0 to lift the Third Division title in 1997 in a dramatic last day. They did, however, also lift the Autoglass Trophy at Wembley two years later.

After several attempts to redevelop Springfield Park – an attractive option owing to its spacious location high above the town – in the late 1980s and early 1990s, the club was instead bought by sports-shop mogul Dave Whelan, who announced plans for it to move to a purpose-built 25,000-seater stadium named after his shop chain – the JJB Stadium. Following the move in 1999 Wigan went on to reach the Premier League in 2005, while Springfield Park was redeveloped as housing; the transformation of club and home was complete.

MEMORIES

I was only young when Springfield Park was around, I was about 11 when it was knocked down but I believe it was one of the main reasons I decided to follow my home town club and not jump on the bandwagons of Manchester United and Liverpool like most of my mates.

The place felt like home, unlike the generic modern stadiums, which just feel like a place to host football matches. I was around seven years old when I started going regularly, during the 1997 promotion season.

My dad used to work so my granddad took me with his mates and I can still remember that match day feeling; walking behind the goals and taking our place in the St Andrews Terrace, which usually involved me dangling my legs over the advertising boards on the halfway line.

My lasting memory will be most people's final memory – the last ever game at the old place when we played Manchester City in the play-offs. We were 1–0 up within about 40 seconds thanks to Stuart Barlow, eventually drawing 1–1. I had my usual 'seat' on the halfway line board and had made a banner to stick there, which went down with the ground.

As the full-time whistle sounded, an air of emotion and sadness rang round the place as thousands poured onto the pitch. I managed to dig myself a bit of the turf up, which still remains in my garden today.

The return of Roberto Martinez was welcomed by Latics fans because with him came back the likes of Graham Barrow and Graeme Jones, old 'Springy Park' favourites, so it felt like a little bit of history and a little bit of that ground we loved was coming back to us.

The place was dirty, old and on its last legs by the end but it played its own key role in making Wigan Athletic the club they are today.

Greg Farrimond

WATSON PETROLEUM
WELCOME TO SPRINGFIELD PARK
PUMA PUMA
BE FIRST FOR LATICS NEWS...
Wigan Evening Post
YOUR ONLY LOCAL EVENING NEWSPAPER
K.W. Golf
01925-638652

PLOUGH LANE – WIMBLEDON

Name:

Plough Lane

Highest attendance:

18,080, vs. HMS Victory,

2 March 1935

First league match:

Wimbledon 3–3 Halifax,

20 August 1977

Final league match:

Wimbledon 0–3 Crystal Palace,

4 May 1991

Memorable moment:

Wimbledon 2–1 Watford,

12 March 1988

(FA Cup quarter-final, en route to final victory)

Current stadium:

Stadium: MK (MK Dons)

Plough Lane was the home of the fabled Wimbledon, the underdog club that enjoyed a meteoric rise up the Football League and into the heart of the nation. Leaving too soon, things were never the same for the club that controversially relocated and changed name, effectively ending any association with history, in 2003.

Wimbledon arrived at Plough Lane as early as 1912. Though they were a very successful and popular amateur side, it would be another 65 years before they would achieve League status.

Upon moving in there was just a wooden grandstand, and 11 years later the club purchased a stand from Clapton (now Leyton) Orient, which they deposited on the south side of the stadium. It was bombed during World War II but restored in time for the 1950–51 season. The Main Stand was replaced in 1957.

Plough Lane played host to many a memorable Wimbledon moment in the 1980s as the club soared from the Fourth Division to the First in just three years, after briefly yo-yoing between Third and Fourth. The side's rise culminated in the famous 1988 FA Cup victory over Liverpool at Wembley.

The Taylor Report recommendations forced Wimbledon to consider their future and, deciding redevelopment would be too costly, they announced a ground share with Crystal Palace, beginning in the 1991–92 season. Three years later then-chairman Sam Hamman sold Plough Lane to Safeway, who attempted unsuccessfully to build a supermarket on the site before selling to housing developers in 2002. Blocks of flats fittingly bear the names of old footballing heroes.

Wimbledon would eventually stay at Selhurst Park until the club's relocation to Milton Keynes in 2003. Plough Lane was where it all went right for Wimbledon, and many think more of an effort could and should have been made to stay there. Instead the stadium - and the club - was eventually lost. AFC Wimbledon, their spiritual successors founded by disaffected supporters, currently play non-League football in Kingston but are seeking to return to the borough.

MEMORIES

Although it is over 60 years since my first visit to Plough Lane as an impressionable five-year-old, it remains indelibly etched in my memory. In 1946 my father returned home from his wartime naval service and, in common with hundreds of thousands of returning young fathers, was eager to develop a relationship with a son whom he didn't know, and – so far as my father was concerned – that meant giving me a love of sport.

We lived in Wimbledon, and so it was natural that my sporting education should begin at our local football club – Wimbledon FC, then playing in the Isthmian League. After a short bus ride from home, we alighted outside the ground, and I can still remember vividly the excitement I felt, being taken to my very first 'proper' match. When viewed through adult eyes, Plough Lane was small, shabby, and neglected, but to me

it was simply magic, and began a love affair with that homely little stadium that lasted until that sad day 56 years later when the club moved to Selhurst Park – sharing with Crystal Palace.

I remember staring in awe at the freshly mown and marked pitch, as we stood on the banking at the Durnsford Road End. The terracing comprised six-inch vertical planks at the front, and steps filled with cinders – it would be a number of years before they were replaced with concrete. The stands were built of corrugated iron, and the seating was simply wooden benches with seat numbers painted along them.

The only adequate description of the gents' ramshackle toilet was 'primitive'. But to men who had spent years at war, these deficiencies were inconsequential. The noise that greeted the players initially frightened me, but I soon drank in the fervour and expectation of the biggest crowd I had even been

in, and I loved it. Within 10 minutes, I had my first football hero – Harry Stannard, the Dons' centre forward.

In fairness there were no hugely significant improvements to Plough Lane over the decades, but I consider myself privileged to have witnessed my humble home town team rise from Isthmian League obscurity to First Division glory, and beat Liverpool to win the FA Cup in 1988. What history was played out in SW19, at that tatty and unprepossessing little stadium, but one thing is for sure, it came to represent the crucible of footballing achievement, and Plough Lane's place in football's history is forever assured.

Tony Thorne

BOROUGH PARK – WORKINGTON AFC

Name:

Borough Park

Highest Attendance:

21,000; v. Manchester United, 4 January 1958

First League Match:

Workington 3-1 Chesterfield, 22 August 1951

Final League Match:

Workington 0-1 Newport County, 14 May 1977

Memorable Moment:

Workington 2-2 Chelsea, 25 November 1964

(League Cup quarter-final)

Current Stadium:

Borough Park

Borough Park is a stadium highly coveted by its tenants – Workington AFC. They took up residence in 1937, a previous incarnation of the club having played at the Lonsdale Park dog track before dissolving in 1911.

A Main Stand on the west side, built when the club moved in, included dressing rooms and offices as Workington set about securing election to the Football League. This was achieved in 1951 and, against the odds, Borough Park would go on to play host to some of the country's elite.

Initial struggles in the Third Division North did not bode well and the club dropped to the Fourth Division on the FA's reshuffling of the League in 1958. But a brief period of success in the 1960s saw not only promotion to the Third Division but a period in which Workington reached League Cup quarter-finals in consecutive seasons as they tangled with West Ham and Chelsea, the latter unable to secure victory when they visited Borough Park.

A near miss on promotion to the Second Division preceded a drop back to the Fourth in 1967; Workington would remain basement-dwellers for a decade before being voted out of the League in 1977 in favour of up-and-coming Wimbledon.

The intervening years have made the stadium look worn. The Main Stand became a casualty of health and safety regulations following the 1985 fire at Valley Parade, and as a result was partially dismantled; the roof and seating were removed, leaving just the changing rooms, offices and restaurant. It created a heavily slanted, unfinished-looking building on the west side.

Opposite is the Popular Side, where the stadium's 500 seats are located. Left of that is the Town End, which is 75 per cent covered by a tin roof running round towards the Main Stand. Directly opposite is the Derwent, or River End, a once-covered goal-side terrace with a grassy bank at the top.

Despite plans for a shared stadium at the adjacent Derwent Park with Rugby League neighbours Workington Town, the football club have remained determined to hang on to their dilapidated home. With recent success leaving them just two promotions away from a return to the Football League, it's not impossible that Borough Park could one day host glamorous football once again.

MEMORIES

As long as I can remember, the first sight of a football ground has been an exciting moment. It doesn't matter if it's the Ajax Arena in Amsterdam, where I was recently, or Borough Park, home of Workington AFC of the UniBond First Division, where I went last Saturday.

The Reds' old stadium, built in 1937, has seen better days. The original floodlight pylons in each corner have been cut down to size for safety reasons and the main stand, which once held over 2,000 people, had its roof removed in 1985, after the Bradford fire disaster.

Underneath the stand, the dressing rooms, treatment room, boiler room, boardroom and sundry other offices remain virtually unchanged. In the draughty corridors, echoes of the past compel the visitor to linger, unhurried, as if in a museum.

'Don't call us Workington Town, that's the rugby club,' warned Steve Durham, whose present titles include match secretary, programme editor and life vice-president. Over the past 40 years, Durham, now 50, has performed dozens of tasks at Borough Park, which include a spell as substitute for the first team when things were really tough in the early 1990s.

Supporters of Workington AFC have many precious memories, none more so than 4 January 1958 when 21,000 crammed into Borough Park for the visit of Manchester United in the third round of the FA Cup. A faded newspaper cutting on the wall under the old stand records the day and the 3-1 defeat for the home side.

After losing Football League status in 1977, Workington became members of the Northern Premier League until 1998 when a further relegation saw the club descend to the North West Counties League. The Reds bounced straight back the following season, however, when a run of 14 straight victories clinched the league championship on the final day, the club's first major title in an existence spanning 115 years.

Borough Park could also get a serious facelift as part of Allerdale Council's plans to regenerate the town centre and maybe next time I go to Workington it will all be very different.

Saturday's home game with Hyde United was postponed but, as I looked out over that lovely old, waterlogged pitch, I was happy just to have been there.

The Daily Telegraph, February 2004

RACECOURSE GROUND – WREXHAM

Name:

Racecourse Ground

Highest attendance:

34,445, vs. Manchester United,

26 January 1957

First league match:

Wrexham 0–2 Hartlepool United,

27 August 1921

Final league match:

Wrexham 1–3 Accrington Stanley,

26 April 2008

Memorable moment:

Wrexham 0–0 Peterborough United,

1 May 1978

(Wrexham lift Third Division title)

Current stadium:

Racecourse Ground

Wrexham's Racecourse Ground may no longer house League football, but its rich history speaks for itself; it is the oldest venue in the world still open to have hosted international football.

It was when Wrexham were elected to the Football League in 1921 that work on the Racecourse Ground really began to pick up; the open terracing behind the goal opposite the famed Kop End was covered by the supporters' club, and a stand was constructed on Mold Road.

It was after World War II that the Kop began to take shape, the supporters themselves laying down the concrete terracing for what would become the largest terrace in the League, holding 4,000 spectators.

In 1962 the club erected a small stand on the terrace, taken from a nearby cinema. It became known as the 'pigeon loft' and lasted just 16 years before it was deemed unsafe; it would be 1980 before the Kop finally received adequate cover.

The 1970s saw the Yale Stand constructed, after the college situated behind it, and the Border Stand erected opposite the Kop. The ground was fully equipped for top-level football and received it in the form of the European Cup Winners' Cup, and saw Wrexham reach the quarter-finals in 1975–76.

The latest modification to the stadium occurred in 1999 with the unveiling of the new Mold Road Stand, a state-of-the-art grandstand with a modern cantilevered roof built in three sections, holding private boxes and even a restaurant.

The stadium looked better than it had in years but events on the pitch weren't going so well as Wrexham were

relegated from the Football League in 2008. The Racecourse Ground had gone from an international venue that raised some eyebrows, to one equipped for such an occasion, yet without a League team inhabiting it. Fans of both the club and the ground will hope that changes in the near future.

MEMORIES

RSC Anderlecht in the European Cup Winners' Cup? Well this is it for me – the big one.– the granddaddy of all European matches at the Racecourse. Wrexham for the first time in their history had reached the quarter-final of the European Cup Winners' Cup.

The first away leg had finished in a narrow 1–0 home win to Anderlecht – I was too young to travel to that match but understood from those that were there that Wrexham were outstanding, particularly Eddie May at the centre of defence and Billy Ashcroft at centre forward and Arfon (Griffiths) and Mel (Sutton) running the midfield.

The home match was set up for a classic; could the Welsh giant killers do it again? The Racecourse was packed to the rafters and the pitch was quite muddy and bobbly.

Owing to the capacity crowd, I was sitting on my Dad's knee in the front row of the upper stand. When Mel Sutton broke

away down the right wing and clipped the ball across to Stuart Lee to slot it home and put us 1–0 my father lost the plot and threw me so high in the air I thought I was going to go head first into the paddock below. For a seven-year-old kid, quite scary at the time.

We put on such a brilliant performance that night, but sadly succumbed to the utter brilliance of Rensenbrink who broke away and slotted the ball astutely out of the reach of the Brian Lloyd. It was to me, bar no other, my greatest memory of Wrexham football club in Europe.
el poncho

BOOTHAM CRESCENT – YORK CITY

Name:
Bootham Crescent

Highest attendance:
28,123, vs. Huddersfield Town,
5 March 1938

First league match:
York City 2–2 Stockport County,
31 August 1932

Final league match:
York City 1–2 Leyton Orient,
1 May 2004

Memorable moment:
York City 3–1 Tottenham Hotspur,
19 February 1955 (FA Cup fifth round)

Current stadium:
Bootham Crescent

York City's move to Bootham Crescent was fan-driven; their former home of just 10 years at Fulfordgate was deemed inaccessible for the City followers as it was too far from the city's railway station. The club took over the stadium from York Cricket Club.

Immediately a main stand was erected and cover was placed over the Popular Side. In 1948 the club purchased the ground after leasing it since their arrival, and supporters immediately went about concreting the Popular Side and Shipton Street terraces.

The share of profit from two FA Cup semi-final ties with eventual winners Newcastle United paid for an extension to the original Main Stand towards the Shipton End in 1955. Further improvements were made to the stadium in 1985 following yet more FA Cup success, including a draw with Liverpool in front of the Bootham Crescent faithful.

The Shipton Street End was renamed in honour of former player David Longhurst in 1990 after he died during a game against Lincoln City. 1994 nearly saw City gain a second successive promotion and enter the First Division, though losing in the play-off semi-finals would be their last taste of League promotion battles. By 1999 they had fallen back down to the basement division. A couple of changes of ownership saw the ground separated from the club, and York were 'half an hour away from oblivion' when the Supporters Trust took them out of administration in March 2003.

City slipped out of the League in 2004, but the Trust were able to steady the ship before giving the majority stake to a businessman and fan with the financial clout to take the club further. Prior to this the club had announced asponsorship deal with locally based confectionery giant Nestle in which the stadium was renamed KitKat Crescent

to the amusement of rival fans. The money the club received for that five-year deal helped them buy back the ground.

The Minstermen have since been working with the City of York Council to find a site for a new stadium to share with York City Knights Rugby League side, and it's hoped this will be the catalyst for the club's future success.

MEMORIES

Chelsea plumb the depths with defeat at York.

In some ways this was a more acutely embarrassing defeat for Chelsea than last Saturday's 6–2 drubbing at home by Nottingham Forest. At least Chelsea were being spanked by the young masters of the First Division three days ago. And they did score twice, something they seldom looked like doing last night.

York, though, are not your everyday hustle-and-bustle thirddivision side. Denis Smith, their manager and former everdependable Stoke City centre-half, is too mindful of how the game should be played to allow the energy to overtake the skill.

Their smart, lively, positive approach has carried them to second place in their division and caused the hairs to rise on bigger scalps than Chelsea in recent years. Twice in the past two seasons Liverpool have only just escaped with their FA Cup lives still intact after drawn games here and Arsenal are one who have perished.

York's goal in the 49th minute came inevitably, with Chelsea's defence caught out of position. Sbragia played the ball into space behind an advanced rearguard and this time Canham, who only turned professional last season at the age of 25, was on side. Avoiding a desperate lunge from Niedzwiecki several yards out of his goal he neatly steered his shot into the far corner of the net while Rougvie, recalled for his first game of the season, could only chaperone the ball home.

***The Times,* September 1986**